THEN AND NOW

BERLIN, 1933 TO NEW YORK, 2004

RUTH LARSON

CHICAGO SPECTRUM PRESS
LOUISVILLE, KENTUCKY 40207

CHICAGO SPECTRUM PRESS
4824 BROWNSBORO CENTER
LOUISVILLE, KENTUCKY 40207
502-899-1919

Printed in the U.S.A.

10 9 8 7 6 5 4 3 2 1

Library of Congress Control Number (LCCN): 2004108000

ISBN: 1-58374-102-X

Recent photo of Ruth Larson by Elana Levy

For Ellen and Daniella

ACKNOWLEDGEMENTS

The support of my family and friends was priceless in getting this book together. I am most grateful to all of them. My daughter, Ellen (Elana) Levy (who read the whole manuscript and made valuable suggestions), my granddaughter, Daniella Salzman, who could not hear enough of my stories, Patty Dann, whose encouragement kept me going, Jacqueline Brown, Mary Davenport, Louise Driver, Margot Fitzgerald, Muriel Manings, Zaphra Rosaki, Sylvia Salem, and Judy Ungar, who all patiently listened to my pieces and rewrites and gave me honest criticism, and Linda Meyer, who typed the whole thing in her free time and made last minute corrections, and Sophie Warning-Peltz, who always said "Write it all down. I want my children to read it one day." Last but not least, I am grateful to my editor, Joyce Engelson, who put it all together and made it real for me. I want to thank you all. Without you, this book would never have been written.

TABLE OF CONTENTS

DORTMUND 1918

I still see myself sitting on top of the kitchen table in our apartment in Dortmund. I was two years old. Next to me stood a big brown stoneware pot filled with butter. I put my hand into the butter and licked my fingers — it was delicious. Hulda had stepped out of the kitchen and I made the most of it, licking my fingers as fast as I could and putting them back into the soft yellow stuff for another sweet lick. When she returned I was completely covered with butter — so the story goes. She proceeded to put a kettle of water on the stove for my unscheduled bath.

I remembered this incident when I was in a restaurant in Puerto Rico in 1995. At the table next to us sat an elegantly dressed couple with their little daughter not more than three years old. She was dressed like a princess, in a white embroidered cotton dress, a gold heart pendant around her neck, gold earrings and a thin gold bracelet. While her parents studied the menu, she was eating the butter with a little breadstick that the waiter had left on the table. By the time the parents were ready to order the butter was completely gone. When the food was served the father offered it to her twice. She vehemently shook her head and did not touch it. When he pushed the plate in front of her she angrily pushed it back, screaming "Nooo." I smiled and looked at the untouched butter on our table. Ever since my husband had his first heart attack, butter no longer appeared on my shopping list.

We lived in Dortmund, a city in the Ruhr valley, until I was five years old. Hulda, a young woman with very long dark brown hair took care of me and the house. She put her long hair up during the day, but when she was in bed her braids touched the floor which occasionally tempted me to pull them up to see how long they were. Hulda lived with us because my mother had to work in the store a block away.

My father had been killed in Rumania in 1917 during World War One. I never knew him. But he knew me. He walked the floor in the living room while I was born in the bedroom, so I was told. I was also told that he came home on furlough once when I was a year old — but I don't remember that. What I do remember is the shooting on the street after the war. The three of us sat in our windowless small hallway, I on my little white chair between the two women. I felt safe. The dark corridor was our safe place. People outside were not only shooting but also throwing stones and breaking windows. We just sat there listening to the scary noise.

"What if they break the windows in the store and steal the merchandise?" my mother murmured.

"They are not interested in kitchenware, they want clothing," Hulda consoled her.

When the noise stopped we went to bed. Hulda went into her room and my mother took me into her bed where I slept as close to her as I could. The crib stood empty at our feet that night.

The store was unharmed.

Once my Aunt Clara, my mother's sister, and my cousin Herta came to visit us. Herta was a year younger than I. We were about two and three years old. Hulda took us on an outing by streetcar. She lifted Herta into the car first and when she bent down to pick me up the tram started moving. My cousin screamed — Hulda yelled and holding on to my hand started running. We made so much noise the conductor waited for us at the next stop.

During the week I went to nursery school every morning, which I liked. I learned to sing and dance and enjoyed showing off my newly acquired skills. Once a neighbor promised me a fresh egg if I would dance for her. I did. Eggs were hard to get at that time and she kept two chickens on her little balcony. I got my egg.

I not only learned to sing and dance; I also caught lice there. When my mother discovered the little crawlers on my head, she immediately bought a remedy. My little white chair was put on top of the kitchen table, the ceiling lamp was pulled down, and the delousing began. Before they put the very poisonous (so I was told) liquid on my head, my mother said, "Close your eyes tightly!" I was not worried about my eyes. I was worried that the deadly fluid would get on my right thumb, my sucking thumb. They wrapped a big towel around my hand — but that was not enough for me. I had to have a pillow on top of the towel. While I held on to the pillow and kept my eyes closed tightly, they put the smelly stuff on my head and killed some of the lice with their fingernails, which made a tiny clicking noise. This procedure became a nightly routine until the lice war was won.

When I was four years old my mother went to a wedding in Berlin. Two unmarried brothers of my father lived there. One was the groom. When she returned she was engaged to the other one, my Uncle Jacob. I had never met him.

It is a Jewish custom that a bachelor brother of the deceased marries the widow. I suppose that was one of the reasons she said "yes." Much later I was told that she did need some encouragement. She got it from the oldest sister of my father. "You know the family, you know we all like you. You won't have a thing to worry about and Ruth gets a good father." I guess that convinced her. It was a good decision.

Uncle Jacob came to Dortmund to visit us. He brought me a beautiful tambourine made of genuine cowhide. I took it to Kindergarten the next morning and let everybody touch it. It was a big success. Nobody had ever seen a tambourine with genuine cowhide.

Our big clock in the living room impressed Uncle Jacob. It chimed every fifteen minutes and he liked the way it sounded. Before he left he told me not to forget to bring it to Berlin. The last months in Dortmund were exciting. I told everybody that "we" were getting married because my uncle liked our clock so much.

The sales lady in Tengelman's, a coffee, tea and candy store, asked me to sell her a curl as a souvenir. I did and was paid with a little tin of violet pastilles, my favorite candy. When we visited Dortmund years after the war, in 1927, the curl was still in the cash register.

The only sad thing about the move to Berlin was that Hulda stayed behind. She did not want to leave Dortmund. A year later she got married and a year after that she had a little girl. She called her Ruth. Uncle Jacob turned smoothly into my father. I called him "Vati." There was never any doubt in my mind or anybody else's that I was his daughter.

BERLIN 1919

I wore a cream-colored sleeveless crepe de chine dress with little crochet buttons on my left shoulder. It was short and loose. I called it my wedding dress — because I wore it to my mother's wedding. It was a big party. There were a lot of people I had never seen before and they were all fussing over me. Admiring my dress, putting their hands through my hair and asking me how I liked Berlin. I was only five years old and this wedding was the beginning of my life in Berlin.

Everything was different here. I had my own room — hot water came out of the faucets in the bathroom and the kitchen. I now took my bath in that big tub instead of in the zinc bowl on the kitchen table. And I had to go to the dentist.

"Open your mouth," he commanded. I had never been in a dentist's office before and it did not look inviting to me.

"Open your mouth, Ruth," my mother chimed in. I just looked at that strange man in white and closed it a little tighter.

"It won't hurt." I was not convinced. For fifteen minutes they unsuccessfully tried to make me open my mouth. In the end my embarrassed mother took me home, my mouth still closed tightly.

My sixth birthday was my first in this big city. I got a lot of presents. But the one thing I really wanted was not among them. "You'll get that big red ball if you stop sucking your thumb," my new father said. I had my eyes on that ball for weeks. I admired it in the store window every day. I wanted that ball. I had to find a way to get it. I stopped sucking my thumb in front of my parents.

Before I entered a room to join them I stood in a corner of the hall and sucked away until my urge was satisfied for the moment. After a week I had perfected this technique. I declared myself clean. I got the ball more for effort than success, I think. It took me another year to conquer this habit completely.

In 1927 when I went to boarding school, I met Berta, 15, who still sucked her thumb. She looked like a Buddha lying on her bed, her thumb in her mouth. The other hand held a big piece of cream colored silk which covered most of her face. That reminded me of my brother Bert. He counted the diapers before he was taken out in his baby carriage. He needed three to suck his thumb. If one was missing he screamed. When they got dirty and my mother wanted to give him clean ones, he screamed too. She could only replace them when he was asleep. He held the three big diapers with both his little hands in front of his face while he was sucking away. He was told to stop and eventually did.

Bert was six years younger than I and had been born in Berlin. I still see my mother leaning against the banister of the staircase with her big belly waiting for my father to take her to the hospital. Not only did I have a new brother, I also had uncles, aunts and cousins I had not known before. My cousin Ingeborg was a year younger but an inch taller than I. I learned to hate her and her family. They lived in a suburb — in a big villa on top of a small hill. Several weekends a year I had to visit her and stay over night. One Sunday we went bicycle riding. I enjoyed it — until her mother ordered me to carry her bike up to the house. I was strong enough to do it but I did not understand why I had to do it. It was not my bike and I was smaller than Ingeborg. The next weekend, after playing outside we each got a piece of fruit. My cousin got a banana. I got a homegrown peach. I was eight years old but I knew that bananas were expensive. For the second time I felt I was not as good a person as Ingeborg. This time I told my parents about it. I did not have to visit her anymore.

I spent most of my free time on the playground in our neighborhood. One day a neighbor informed my mother that I was sitting on a lamppost in the playground. "She should have been a boy," my mother murmured. It was not the only time she said that. When I practiced headstands behind closed doors in the apartment, I could hear her mumbling, "She should have been a boy."

Gym was my favorite subject in school. I excelled in it. I was a particularly good jumper and could outrun anyone in my class, boy or girl. The gym teacher could not complain about my accomplishments. However one day she did find something to complain about.

"You cannot wear political insignias in school!" She had seen my new necklace with a Jewish star pendant. I had gotten it on my eleventh birthday.

"It's not a political insignia," I said.

"Take it off, you cannot wear it in my class."

I did not excel in my scholastic work.

"Ruth cannot sit still. She does not concentrate on her work."

It was the constant complaint my mother heard from my teachers. She started to bribe me. Every time I got a good grade in some class work, she gave me a little toy. She had an entire collection of small toys locked up in her closet. I liked them and wanted them but did not always succeed. In desperation she took me to our pediatrician. He came up with the perfect prescription for me.

"She needs more outlets for her surplus energy. The gym in school is not enough."

I was registered in an after school class for additional athletics two days a week. I was the smallest in that class but could hold my own in jumping.

"Your daughter has a spring in her belly," the teacher told my mother. I don't know how my mother felt, but I was very proud. I still had three afternoons for the playground. At age eleven I did not sit on lampposts anymore. Now I played marbles. I put two blue and two brown ceramic ones into my pouch — that was all I wanted to risk. A few hours later my sack was filled to the brim and I went home. One evening I proudly showed my father the spoils of the day.

"You took the marbles away from poor children. You have to give them back."

"I did not take them away. I won them."

"Give them back!"

I was proud of my winnings and he made me feel like a thief. I did not give them back. The next day I put my winnings quietly into my big sack in the toy chest.

Bert and I shared a room until he was three years old. It was in the front of our apartment — close to my parents' bedroom. The maids had their quarters at the other end. At least one of them was always in the house when my parents went out. We were never left alone. I once heard my father say, "The apartment never stays alone." When we were two and eight years old, I started to get tense when my parents went out in the evening. I was not worried about my safety; I worried about their safety. I could not fall asleep until they were home. I began to use magic in order to get them home. Since my bedroom door, at my request, had to stay open, I could see the light going on and off in the stairway through a small window in our entrance door. When you entered the building you turned the light on. It would turn itself off automatically after a short while. So I could see from my bed whenever someone entered the house. I knew what time it was because I heard the chimes from the clock in the dining room. When it rang eleven times I started worrying. I began to count how often the lights went on in the stairwell. They had to be back by the third light. If that did not work the first time, I would start counting the lights again. The magic usually worked the second time. When they finally looked in on us, I made believe I was asleep and was doubly happy if my mother gave me a gentle kiss.

One night, however, nothing worked. They did not come home after the second count. The chimes in the dining room rang twelve times. I was sure something had happened to them. I had to do something more daring. All I could think was "please come home!" In desperation I even started praying. It did not help. I proceeded to turn the lights on; ceiling lights, table lamps, floor lamps in every front room. Our windows now were brightly lit and very visible from the street. I went back to my room and waited. It worked! They were home within ten minutes. I don't know if they were upset when they saw the apartment brilliantly illuminated. But I do remember how relieved I was when I heard the key in the lock. I did not pretend to be asleep. I was ready to face the punishment. I did not care. They were home, that was all I cared about. My mother came quietly into our room, kissed Bert, told me to go to sleep, closed the door and did not kiss me.

The next morning I was told to write, "I will fall asleep when my parents go out at night" one hundred times. When my daughter started going out I stayed awake until she was home. I did not use any magic to get her back. I just worried and resented my husband who was sound asleep and left the agonizing to me.

THE CROSS 1923

One spring day my parents decided to take my brother Bert, age three, and me, age nine, on their yearly trip to Bad Kissingen. That they took us along was a consequence of the pork dinner incident. They had left us at home the year before with two competent maids and an aunt who checked on us daily. At night, I did my own checking. I tiptoed through the dining room and the long dark hallway in my nightgown and listened for sounds behind the maids' closed doors. Only then could I sleep peacefully. All went well until we were offered pork roast for dinner. I knew it was pork because it was all fat. I did not eat it. "This is pork!"

"Yes, try it. It is good." I refused and would not let Bert eat it either. We did not have a kosher household, but pork never entered our kitchen. I told my aunt about it. We were never left alone again.

Bad Kissingen was and still is a typical spa resort. It looked much like the town in "Last Year in Mariendbad," with manicured lawns and beautifully tended flower gardens. A music shell stood in the middle of this park-like town. People would promenade around it in the afternoon with their fancy "Bad Kissingen" engraved glasses, drinking the local spring water, which had a magic healing power. All this took place in slow motion. They walked slowly and drank the waters even more slowly, while the band played older people's favorite music. Not an ideal vacation spot for children! My parents engaged a young woman, Grete, to take care of us during the day. She came after breakfast and stayed with us till dinner. I don't remember where we had lunch, but I know that we went for dinner to the big dining room every night. Fresh flowers on every table, the snow-white tablecloths, shining silver, and music, all made for a glamorous and intimidating experience. I always held my mother's hand when we walked to our table. The guests were all dressed in their finest. My mother wore a cornflower blue dress, my father put on a different tie every evening. Bert wore his little blue suit and a tie made to order for him. I remember my favorite dress, which my father had brought me from Vienna. It was bright red with blue embroidery in a chessboard pattern around the front and a white collar. I wore white knee socks and black patent leather shoes.

Grete came every morning and took us out for walks. One day we went in a new direction. This uphill path led into the woods. Everything went fine, until on the left side the first stop of a *Passionsweg* appeared. It was a wooden box the size of an orange crate mounted on wooden stilts, but not too high for both adults and children to see inside. It was like a doll house with little painted figures of people and animals. It presented the birth of Jesus.

I knew about the *passionsweg* and started to feel uncomfortable. I knew there would be more boxes to come, presenting different stages of Christ's life. At the end would be a larger-than-life cross. Where could I have seen this before? I don't know to this day, but I knew the big cross would come and I was afraid of it — very much afraid.

"Grete, is there a cross coming?"

"No, no cross."

"Grete, I am afraid of crosses. There is one coming, I know! Let's go back!" She shook her head, took my hand, and pulled me around. With every station we passed I became more upset.

"Grete, please let's turn around. The cross is coming!"

But she walked on. I tried to pull her around but couldn't. I closed my eyes, then opened them for a split second to see if the inevitable was coming. I knew it would appear soon and started crying and begging her to turn around.

"Grete, let's go back. I don't want to see it, please!"

I opened my eyes again. Among the trees a huge cross was rising, glittering in the sun. I started screaming and used all my strength to pull away from her. "There it is!" I turned around and ran as fast as I could down the hill. It was even worse for me to have the cross behind me. I looked back to see if it might be following me. Grete was running after me holding Bert in her arms. But she could not catch me. I cried all the way to the hotel until I found my mother.

I don't know how Grete explained the incident, and I don't remember if there were any consequences for her. All I remember is the horror. That night I slept in my mother's bed.

This phobia stayed with me for a long time. Whenever we traveled and I found a cross over my bed in a hotel, my mother had to take it off the wall and out of the room.

At age fifteen I went on a camping trip to Italy. No getting away from entering churches here. Bravely I went in, stayed behind, let the group inspect it, and sneaked out as soon as I could. I did not want anybody to know about this irrational fear. I have tried to find the source of this phobia. But all I can remember is that incident with Grete.

I began fighting it. The problem was not so much to go into a church and look at the cross, the problem was to get out. When I had my back to the cross, the anxiety would start. I began to use one of the side aisles to get out if I could not find a side door.

Since then I have been in many churches, admired them and even loved some. I don't have to look for a side door any more. However, I doubt whether I could sleep peacefully with a cross over my bed. I eat ham and love bacon, but when it comes to pork roast, I pass.

SHORT VACATIONS

On short vacations I frequently went to visit relatives. When I was ten years old I went with my mother to Elberfeld, a day's train ride from Berlin. We visited Uncle Hugo and his family, Aunt Jenny, their two sons, Ludwig and Kurt, and a maiden Aunt Rosalie, who, like Jenny, was my father's sister. Rosalie, my oldest aunt, was also the strictest. To show her love for me and my two younger cousins, Ilse and Ursel in Berlin, she knitted the most awful dresses in triplicate every year. We all hated them. The most unforgettable was dirndl-style. It had a dirty teal color top. The skirt had vertical stripes: red, brown, green, yellow, blue and the awful teal. I only had to wear it when she came for her half-yearly visits to Berlin. However, many years later, in 1938, before I left Germany, she came to Berlin and knitted two beautiful sweaters for me. One was red, the other moss green. The red one I loved and wore for many years.

Kurt was my favorite cousin and the main reason I longed to go to Elberfeld. We were inseparable and slept in the same room. One rainy day I decided to jump down a whole flight of stairs in their house. Kurt tried to discourage me but I jumped anyway and landed with a big thud. My aunt came running and gave us both hell. I did not confess that it was all my fault. When he was fifteen years old, he and his older brother Ludwig went for a vacation to a small town on the Rhine. In trying to measure the depth of the river, Ludwig fell in. Kurt jumped in to save him. Ludwig managed to get to shore but Kurt drowned. His body was found in Holland weeks later and brought back to Elberfeld. We went to his funeral. I never had been to a funeral and was afraid. Seeing all the adults cry scared me even more. I kept my eyes on the ground and stayed close to my mother who had her arm around me. I was glad when we went home. I did not want to think about it anymore.

I also spent many vacations with my cousins at the farm of my mother's sister, Clara. Heinz was two years older, Herta a year younger, and Mirjam was a baby. Every noon Herta and I would ride on big workhorses to the fields to bring lunch to the workers. We loved it. Our feet stuck out horizontally from the big animals like toothpicks. It was wonderful riding on the cobblestone streets through the little village. We were up so high we could look down on the tiny old houses.

Among all the farm animals it was the billy goat that nearly got the better of me. Maybe I had teased him, I don't remember. What I do remember is that the beast suddenly tried to charge me with his horns. He came at me like a bull. I ran into the house. He ran into the house. I ran up the stairs and he ran up the stairs. I got into the bedroom and slammed the door. He banged at the door with his horns. I screamed out the window and Heinz came to my rescue. He took him by the horns and led him down the stairs, out of the house and into the stable.

It was my last summer vacation with relatives. The following year, at age 12, I was sent to a co-ed summer camp near Berlin. I enjoyed competing with the boys in the games we played, like Voelkerball, a two team ball game where I had no trouble scoring a goal. I enjoyed my stay; it was a happy experience. However, after four weeks I was looking forward to seeing my parents again, even though I dreaded going back to school.

I was thirteen and in high school but my scholastic work showed no improvement. My parents decided to send me to a boarding school. I was not involved in the decision. But when I was told that in April, at the start of the new term, I would go to the "Schule am Meer" (the school on the sea) on the island Juist, I was thrilled. How they got the idea of sending me to a boarding school I don't know. I also don't know how they found this particular one. But I was not upset. I had been in a camp during my last summer vacation and enjoyed it. I thought it would be a camp with classes. I was curious and, in a hesitant way, looking forward to it. The preparations — sewing name tags not only into all my clothing and underwear but also onto new wool blankets, sheets and towels — added to the excitement. With two large suitcases my mother and I left for the long trip from Berlin to Juist. It was a day's train ride from Berlin to Nordeich. From there we took a boat and reached the island two hours later.

ARRIVAL IN JUIST 1927

We could see the island coming closer. It was a long narrow piece of land, part of a chain of islands on the northern coast of Germany. Norderney was the most famous, a well-known summer resort, right next to Juist, with fancy hotels and prestigious children's camps. Juist was its poor cousin, a less expensive resort.

When we got off the boat we piled into a little train that pulled us over a high trestle to the tiny station. Shortly before reaching it, the little train slowed down and squeaked and squealed around a sharp curve. It went so slowly that we students came to call it the flower picking train. There were no flowers to pick but you could have gotten off, picked a bouquet and reboarded without any difficulty. Coming back after a vacation the squeaking and squealing would be the cue to throw our hand luggage off the train and jump after it. It was a short cut to the school. We students could only jump at low tide when the ground was dry. Sometimes we miscalculated and landed with a big splash.

On this first arrival, we walked from the station behind the horse-drawn cart that carried everybody's luggage. There were no cars on the island. It was a good half hour walk to the school. First through the village with its cobblestone streets, then along a sandy path through the dunes. The cart moved slower on the sand, the suitcases noisily swaying from side to side. I was waiting for some to fall off — but none did.

Nobody talked to us. After a while my mother and I were the only ones left behind the carriage. Everyone else was walking in front of the horse. Suddenly I realized I was not going to a summer camp! Will I be able to do my homework here? It was scary. I glanced at my mother. She seemed buried in her own thoughts. Suddenly she turned her head and smiled at me. I smiled back. I felt better.

Walking through the village we had passed Bering's bakery. Later, when I was a student, on Saturday afternoons four or five of us would walk to the village and go into this little store to pounce on their delicious apple cake waiting for us on a big tray on the counter. It was not that we did not get enough to eat — we were just always hungry. Sometimes at night we would invade the kitchen through an open window in the basement. We ate anything: cold porridge, dry bread, cold soup.

Every other week we were allowed a package from home, but fruit only. No other food could be mailed — except on birthdays. Then we could get a "Fresspaket." Mine was filled with pastramis, cheese, cake, cookies, chocolates, dried fruit and candy. Everyone came to celebrate, and that delicious food was gone in no time.

On this first walk to the school I was not hungry. I was eager to get there. A waiting teacher greeted us warmly and introduced me to my roommate Brigitte. She, my mother, and I went up to our room on the second floor of the main building. On the first floor were the dining room and teachers' offices. There were four buildings around a big yard, the two-story main building and two one-story houses, which we called barracks. In one were the sleeping quarters of the younger boys, in the other one were the two big shower rooms, the toilets, the laundry and a big utility room. On the fourth side was the "Ark" another two-story building. It was occupied by the three upper classes. Boys downstairs, girls upstairs. The two last years before graduation we each had our own room in the Ark.

Brigitte and I silently started unpacking. My mother sat on the bed watching us. From the corner of my eyes I scrutinized my roommate. She was looking at me too. But we did not talk.

"I'll take the upper berth," I finally said.

"OK with me. I don't like to climb anyway."

One night Brigitte heard squeaking and tiny foot patter in the drawer under her bed. We had a mouse. We did not dare to open the drawer. Instead we told some boys about it at breakfast.

"I'll get rid of it for you," Tom, age fifteen, said. "I'll come up after lunch."

He did and pulled out a little revolver, opened the drawer and killed the mouse with one shot. He picked it up by its tail and waved it in front of our faces. We did not dare to scream, just pushed him out the door, the dead mouse dangling from his hand.

A total of eighty students attended the school; two thirds were boys. We were a closed community, living by our own rules, having nothing to do with the village. Ours was an honor system but nobody called it that. Occasionally rules were stretched to the breaking point, like walking on the beach after curfew or turning the light out too late. One rule however was never broken: nobody ever went into the ocean without supervision.

Our day was entirely structured. At 6:30 a.m. Lu, the director, woke us up singing "Rise, rise, rise." Then we rushed into the dunes for fifteen minutes of gymnastics and down to the beach into the ocean for a short mandatory dip. (In the fall and winter this dip was voluntary.) With bathrobes over our wet swimming suits, we ran up the dunes to be the first under the hot shower.

In the summer we went for a longer swim before lunch. Two teachers about sixty meters apart represented an imaginary rope. Short people had an imaginary rope when the water reached their rib cage. At low tide the ocean left big deep pools behind. I learned how to swim in these pools.

At 8 a.m. a hungry crowd rushed into the dining room where the sweet smell of hot porridge tickled our noses and stomachs. However, before we could sit down we had to stand behind the tables and listen to a prelude and fugue by Bach, which Zuck our music teacher played on the harpsichord. A different prelude and fugue every morning — all forty-eight of them. Sometimes the sweet smell became too much for a hungry boy and he would silently slide down against the wall and collapse. Nobody paid attention to him. That was how my first day started too. It began with gym, my favorite subject.

After breakfast the regular school day started. We went into our classrooms and the teachers joined us. After lunch one hour and a half was set aside for homework.

When the tide was low the beach was so wide and the sand so hard that it made an ideal playing field for hockey. I learned the game fast. Once we played against a school from the mainland, the only time we engaged another team. I was the only girl on the field. We won!

Besides hockey we practiced all the track and field events. I excelled in the hundred-meter dash and in broad jumping. By the time I was fifteen, some boys were faster than I but none of the girls.

On this first evening Zuck gave a piano concert to which my mother was invited. It was tradition to have a musical evening the first night after a vacation. (We had three vacations a year, four weeks each.) Every Monday night we listened to music. If Zuck did not play for us the school orchestra with or without the choir would perform. I joined the choir. We all enjoyed singing, particularly canons and would often sing them among ourselves.

The subject of religion never came up. I knew a few students who were Jewish but most of my friends were not. My parents had always kept me informed about the Jewish holidays but we never observed them at school. Except for one year when Yom Kippur fell on a weekend. That year my friend Gertrud and I decided to go to Norden, the closest little town on the mainland. We thought of it more as an adventure than a holiday. On Saturday we took the boat and the train for a short ride to Norden. And rented a cheap room for two nights. The next morning we went to the little synagogue. Two families promptly invited us for dinner that night to break the fast. We had secretly counted on that. However, fasting was hard for us. We started walking out of the little town, bought two large pickles and ate them where no one could see us. We were still hungry but did not dare to eat anything else. We decided a pickle does not count, we were still fasting.

We went back to the synagogue in time for the end of the service. And I went home with my hosts. Their living room served as the dining room that night.

"Sit down, we'll just wash up and will be right back."

I sat at the festive, decorated table. On the white tablecloth were white dishes with a big blue flowery border. On every big plate sat a smaller matching one with a piece of sweet smelling challah tickling my nose and teasing my stomach. I was starving. I started to pick the raisins out of the challah on my plate and eat them. But it did not help much. By the time the family came back I had picked the raisins out of every piece of challah on the table. The candles were lit and the dinner was served. Not a word about the missing raisins.

My parents were happy that for once I had observed a holiday. They observed all the high holidays. However, holidays were not on my mother's mind this first evening in the school. She had enjoyed the concert and we were quietly walking to the little inn next to the school, the only house in this part of the island that was not attached to the school. I brought her up to her room and then walked slowly back and up to my room. Brigitte seemed to be asleep. Carefully I climbed into my bunk. I was tired and restless. School will start tomorrow — will I be able to do the work? What will my classmates be like? Other than Brigitte I had not met anybody. My mother will leave in the morning. She is going back and Berlin is far away. It was scary but also exciting. Once she is gone I'll be on my own, really on my own.

The next morning I was standing on top of the stairs getting ready for my first class when my mother called me down to say good-bye. She held me for a long time and I was holding on to her too.

"Don't worry about me," I finally said.

"Don't forget to write," were her parting words.

"I won't." Then we walked out the door where the little horse drawn cart was waiting to take her to the station. We waved to each other and I watched her slowly disappear.

LIFE ON JUIST

Life in the Schule Am Meer agreed with me. I liked it. The day was structured. All our classes were in the morning. Nothing was scheduled for an hour and a half after lunch. We used this time to visit each other or to do homework. Two afternoons we played hockey on the beach — weather and tides permitting (we could only play at low tide). Three afternoons we worked on the grounds, particularly around the New Music Hall. Dirt had to be brought to the new building, and little squares of grass were carefully laid to become a new lawn. At other times we would plant flowers. We always had beautiful tulips in the spring, which bloomed in every color from white to a very dark purple, nearly black, which made the yard look like a painter's palette.

One morning the beach was covered with hundreds of perfectly cut logs. Classes were cancelled. Everybody, students and teachers, had to collect the wood and put it into a big pile on the beach. Two people had to guard the pile at all times. Stranded goods belonged to everybody and the people living on the island were as eager as we were to collect it. Before the sun went down we each put one log over our shoulder and crawled up the dunes to start a new pile in the school yard. We built a little house with these logs, it became a classroom and was called Gaurisankar. I don't remember where this exotic name came from.

Sometimes an afternoon was interrupted by a dogfight. Robby, a big black Newfoundland who looked like a bear, just waddled slowly around the yard, not interested in the other dogs or any humans. We kept our distance from him because he smelled god-awful. But Hector, Zuck's German Shepherd and Korf, Tante Mia's German Shepherd-like dog, hated each other. Tante Mia was in charge of the school kitchen. They tried not to let them roam around at the same time but did not always succeed. These dogs would lock their teeth into the enemy's throat and not let go. Some of the older and bigger boys would try to pull them apart but a pail of cold water poured over their heads was the only way to stop the fight. Then Tante Mia and Zuck would pull their bleeding dogs home but not before they gave each other a disgusted glance implying, "it was your fault." The smaller one, Korf, was always hurt the most but he was the instigator every time. Once he lost part of an ear, another time his leg was injured so badly that he started limping, but these injuries did not stop Korf from picking the next fight.

When nothing was scheduled for the evening we frequently went for a walk on the beach. Once six of us started out on a moonlit night. It was low tide and we walked on the hard sand talking and singing. Suddenly we were surrounded by dense fog. We could not see the dunes or the two lights that indicated the path leading to the school. We were standing on an island. On one side was the ocean, on the other a pond formed by the outgoing tide. We did not know which was which. After a short discussion we agreed on the direction, took our shoes off and waded through the water. After a few tense moments we landed on the beach. It was a scary experience.

One summer night I went for a walk with Anne, my classmate and friend,. Again the tide was low and the sand hard and the moon bright. The beach and the ocean looked like an eerie landscape in the bluish light. We walked for a long time. Suddenly it was 10:30 p.m. We realized that we could never be back by eleven, the curfew for the upper classes. Since we could not be back on time we decided to walk around the east end of the island and come back on the marsh side. We had no idea how long it would take us since we had never taken this walk before. We arrived at the school at 2 a.m. Trying to sneak into our building we ran into Dr. Reiner. Next to the director he was the most important but also the most feared teacher. He was the only teacher who was addressed by his name. All the others had nicknames. The Director Lu's real name was Luserke, Zuck's real name was Zuckmeyer, etc. Why he was in the yard at this hour was a mystery to us. He did not have to cross the big court to go to the bathroom. His apartment had inside plumbing. He confronted us, gave us a lecture on the rules and regulations of the school (as if we did not know them), adding: "Go to bed, I'll talk to you tomorrow."

Back in my room I considered myself lucky. If I had been with my boyfriend instead of with Anne, the consequences could have been serious. Only a few weeks earlier, Ralph was caught coming out of Gerda's room at midnight. Not only did we have an eleven o'clock lights out rule but after 9 p.m., no visitors of the opposite sex were permitted. Ralph had also run into Dr. Reiner. It seemed that he roamed around the school at night waiting for someone to break the rules. A good looking, married man, he was also flirtatious. Rumor had it that he was more than flirtatious with Cathy, an upper-class student. Ralph and Gerda had to pack their suitcases in the morning and leave the school for good on the next boat. Our punishment: for one week we had to be in our rooms at 9 p.m. In addition we had to push a wheelbarrow loaded with dirt for one hour every afternoon for a week.

Our extra-curricular activities were confined to the beach at night, until Ruprecht, a classmate and I started dances on Saturday night. We both liked to dance and danced well together. He had a record player and lots of records. We cleared out one classroom and danced. It became a popular activity and on request Rup and I started giving dancing lessons. He taught the boys and I the girls. I loved it. It became our regular Saturday night entertainment during the winter.

In the summer Juist was a resort and the big hotels held afternoon tea dances. One Saturday afternoon Ruprecht, his girlfriend Rita and Hans, my boyfriend and I decided to go to the tea dance at the Strand Hotel. The boys wore their knickerbocker pants. We girls put our only cotton dresses on. They were all the same cut, only a different color. Mine was pink and Rita's was yellow. They were straight buttoned down dresses. We wore them only on special occasions. Rita and I wore white socks and low-heeled oxfords, the fanciest shoes we had. We walked forty-five minutes through the dunes and over cobblestones to the hotel, sat down at a table, ordered a lemonade each, and danced non-stop until the band left the stage. Then we rushed back to the school to be in time for dinner. For several weeks it was our regular Saturday afternoon entertainment, until one day the school got a call from the Strand Hotel. "Your students dance indecently," they complained. Apparently we dipped too low dancing the Tango. That was the end of those excursions.

I did well scholastically and was advanced every year. Two years before graduation I got my own room as did all my upper-class mates. The room was small and furnished with a bed, a desk, a bookshelf and a built-in closet. We could decorate it ourselves. I had a pretty blue bedspread, a Van Gogh picture on the wall and a vase with wild flowers on my desk. Van Gogh was all the rage. Everyone had a Van Gogh on the wall, mostly the sunflowers and so did I. In addition I had the Blue Horses by Marc over my bed.

During our last year we all started to study more seriously. We had graduation in front of us, which entailed a written and oral exam. We still participated in all activities but our free time was now dedicated to studying. Sometimes Hilde, my classmate and close friend, and I would sit together and rehearse questions that might come up. Or I would rehearse math questions with her. She was better in that subject than I. We all realized that these exams were a serious matter and tried to help each other as much as we could.

THE BIG FREEZE

The temperature was below zero Celsius. The bay was frozen solid. Dr. Reiner was sick. No mail, no food, no supplies. No medication. It was the first time that the school had been totally cut off from the mainland. Classes took place, meals were served. Tante Mia had filled the pantry for emergencies. The students thought it was all very romantic and exciting. We did not worry — not even about Dr. Reiner whose illness was talked about in whispers. However, when the one and only physician on Juist, Dr. Fenshel suddenly appeared on his bicycle we realized that something was seriously wrong. Nobody had ever consulted Dr. Fenshel. Nobody took him seriously. We called him the "Viehdoctor" (veterinarian), Frau Haffner, a registered nurse, the wife of one of the teachers, took care of our colds and other complaints. No student ever got seriously ill. When we saw this tall thin man, fisherman's cap on his head, a satchel on the handle bar, pedaling into the school yard, he looked like a circus performer. They must have called for him in desperation.

At dinner that night we were informed that classes for the next day were canceled. The tide was low at 10 a.m. A plane would come from Norderney, the island next to Juist. It would bring mail, supplies and medication. With red theater curtains and multi colored bedspreads we outlined a landing area on the hard sand. Then we all stood on the dunes, waiting. Finally the little flying machine flew over the outlined area at low altitude, turned around and went back to Norderney. We ran down to the beach to make the runway longer — and up again — waiting. Ten minutes later the plane landed. We raced toward the little machine as if it had come from outer space. It was a special event, the first time a plane had landed on Juist, and we had made it possible. Then we started unloading it. I was mostly interested in the mail. For ten days we had been without news from home.

The most important package was the medication for Dr. Reiner. His brother-in-law, a physician who lived in Zurich, had made the diagnosis via telephone and arranged for the medication to be flown to Norderney.

Dr. Fenshel came again on his bicycle and gave Dr. Reiner the prescribed injection. We now knew that he was seriously ill. For a few days they considered flying him to Zurich. Then his condition improved and that plan was canceled. Unfortunately the weather did not also improve. Parents were called and reassured that our rooms were warm and that we had enough to eat. At dinner that evening, Lu, the director, announced again that there would be no classes the next day. Instead we would all, student and teachers, walk across the ice to the mainland, pick up supplies and carry them home in our backpacks.

Not all teachers went along. Aeschli, the math teacher to the lower classes, and his wife whom we called Aeschlimiss stayed behind. They were older and not too steady on their feet. Aeschli used to sit in front of the class, sharpening one of his pencils with his pocketknife, while giving us an exercise in adding and subtracting. Three plus ten, minus four plus eleven, on and on it went. We had to make the calculations in our heads. Suddenly he would stop and ask us what the final number was. Every class started that way. Aeschlimiss taught English. She was good. I learned the irregular verbs well. I still sometimes recite them in my head.

Of course, all the young teachers came along. There was Dr. Rittmeyere. He was Swiss and we called him Ritterly. A small man who taught history, he had a hard time asserting himself. His room was in a long one-story building where the younger boys lived. One day he opened the door to his room and the ass of our only horse was staring him in the face.

And Mr. Epper joined, in his black corduroy pants. He wore these pants every day for weeks. One night two boys sneaked into his room and swiped them. The next morning, Mr. Epper was sick. He got the pants back in the afternoon and recovered immediately.

At 8 a.m. the next morning we started walking. In front of us was a grayish-white landscape — ice. There was no horizon. The grey sky blended into the ice. No land in sight. Lu, compass in hand was leading the pack. He looked like a sailor with his captain's hat and well-worn windbreaker. He did not wear his usual black skullcap, which looked like a yarmulke. The story was that he had been wounded in World War One and had to keep his head covered at all times. We often wondered what he wore in bed. A white nightcap with ribbons tied around his neck? His famous long pipe was missing on this outing too. The pipe's head was porcelain and elf-like women in pink and blue veils were painted on it. The pretty porcelain head was always resting on the floor. He dropped a lighted match into it to get it started. He never missed his target.

He did take the pipe along, however, when he sailed with a few of us to Norderney one summer. The purpose of that trip was to teach us sailing. The only thing I remember is that I had to go to the bathroom. There were no facilities on board. I envied the boys who just stood at the railing with their backs to me and peed. I had to wait until we finally got to Norderney.

Once my roommate and I acted like boys. We lived on the second floor of the main house. The dining room was below us. It was in the evening and dark. We were too lazy to walk across the big yard to the bathrooms. We positioned ourselves on the windowsills, held on to the frames, and peed.

After a three-hour walk we finally arrived in Nordeik. By now the sun had come out. The ice was glistening with little diamonds and the sky was blue. The little harbor was filled with motionless boats. It was an eerie sight as they were perfectly still, not even their masts swayed. An army of boats standing at attention. We walked past them and climbed a little ladder to reach land.

In a small restaurant a pre-ordered lunch was waiting. The food and the hot tea were enough to refresh us. But we did not have much time to rest. We had to be home before dark. Oatmeal, flour, sugar, fruit and potatoes stood neatly packed in a corner. I took a bag of oatmeal and put it into my backpack. I left the heavier packages for the boys. Once all the packages were loaded on our backs we started on our long trek home, Lu leading us again. He walked a little slower and so did we. It was a silent group. My load got heavier with every step. I walked like a robot putting one foot in front of the other. My boyfriend Hans took my hand and pulled me silently along. But as Juist loomed bigger and bigger in the distance, our steps became faster. We reached the island just before sunset. It had taken us four hours to get home.

The next morning we were permitted to sleep an hour longer. The usual pre-breakfast gym was canceled. Dr. Reiner resumed teaching after two weeks. He finished the term. For the Easter vacation he went to Zurich. He died of cancer in Switzerland four months later.

CAMPING TRIP

Five of us were left for the long hike from Riva to Laredo. The other five were "invalids." They had painful blisters on their feet and insisted on taking the bus and would meet us in Laredo the next morning.

We were on a ten-day camping trip through northern Italy. It was part of the curriculum of the Schule Am Meer. I had a blister on my foot too, but I refused to give in to it. With the help of a special ointment and a band-aid I kept on walking.

I had little sympathy with the invalids. During my first camping trip the year before, at age thirteen, I would have welcomed belonging to the invalids — but not because of blisters. Two days before that trip to a little mountain range near Berlin, my very first period appeared. I was at home; these camping trips started after our summer vacation. My mother refused to let me go. She argued that I could hurt myself for life. I argued that we were only two girls and if I could not go Lore couldn't go either. Dr. Kopf, the leader, would not take eight boys and one girl on the trip. In desperation she called our family doctor.

"Let her go," he said, "it won't do her any harm."

We walked 25 kilometers a day. I was sore every step of it. After a few days Dr. Kopf had pity on me and carried my heavy knapsack on top of his. It helped a little but not much.

On this trip to Italy we were also eight boys and two girls plus Zuck, our leader, who spoke Italian. I belonged to Zuck's close circle. There were twelve of us. We had our meals together and met for tea and cookies every Sunday afternoon in his little apartment. We went to him when we got into trouble or had a problem. Many years later, long after I had graduated and the school did not exist anymore, we happened to be in Munich on the same day. We arranged to meet at the railway station. Zuck saw me coming, stretched out his arms, I started running.

"The Mohr is here. How are you, little Mohr?" My nickname was Mohr, which means "Moor" (Othello was a Moor), because my hair was black and curly. It felt good to see him after so many years. We had lunch together and then he boarded his train back to Ankara where he taught music. It was the last time I saw him. He died two years later in Turkey.

On this trip to Italy, he was full of pep and walked better than any of us. We had spent the night before in our tents in a vineyard. The owner of the vineyard had given us permission to eat as many grapes as we wanted. They were so filling that I could not even finish half a bunch to my great regret. We preferred to sleep in hay barns in our primitive sleeping bags, wool blankets sewn together on three sides. The hay was warm and soft, if frequently itchy.

In the morning we five able bodies, including Zuck, started on our long hike to Laredo. The road was along vineyards. The ripe grapes teasingly dangled over the fence to our left. We tried to reach them but they were so high that even when the tall boys jumped they could not touch them. We did not give up, our eyes were glued to the unreachable fruit. Nobody even glanced to the right where the blue lake Garda was glittering in the sun. Zuck suddenly screamed, "Look to the right — at the lake! I did not take you on this trip to figure out how to steal fruit!" Nobody had seen the lake.

After a long day we arrived at the little village late in the afternoon, tired and hungry. My blister had started acting up and we all walked a little slower. We were looking forward to some food and a warm hay barn. Zuck discovered a village tavern. The proprietor, a little round woman with a slightly spotted white apron had no hay barn but she did have rooms to rent. That sounded even better. First, however, we wanted to eat. She led us into her tavern and seated us at a freshly polished wooden table, served us wine and disappeared into the kitchen to make the pasta. Slowly the room filled with men who had obviously come from work for their afternoon drink. They looked at us and we smiled at them. Suddenly they began to sing, smiling back at us. We clapped when they stopped and answered them by singing a canon. Then they clapped and started singing again, and on it went until we left and everybody said, "ar rivederci."

The proprietor led us across a cobblestone yard to a small building. I began to fantasize about a shower or maybe even an inside toilet? It was not exactly ideal to always hide behind a tree in the woods where little things were crawling around.

First, however she pointed to a little hut — the outhouse! We immediately stood in line to use it. Nobody wanted to enter that little hut alone during the night. She proceeded to lead us up a steep flight of stairs. There were several doors on the landing. She opened one. A huge bed with sparkling white linen appeared. Standing next to it was a white enameled bowl with matching ewer on a washstand. There was just enough space on one side of the bed to get into it — the other side was flush against the wall. Our hostess pointed at two of the boys and said, "Two sleep here."

Then she opened the second door. That room was the identical twin of the first one. She pointed to the remaining two males — one was Zuck — "this is for you," she said.

"I get my own room!" I fantasized. But then she pointed at me and addressed Zuck, "She has to sleep with my daughter."

"In your daughter's room?" Zuck asked.

"No, in the big bed with her." I did not utter a word. I just looked desperately at Zuck. I was not going to sleep with any stranger's daughter in one bed. Zuck knew it. He looked at me, "You have your choice. You can sleep with her daughter in one bed, or you can share the bed with Ralph and me."

"I sleep with you," shot out of my mouth. The lady smiled and left the room. Zuck slept in the middle. Ralph pushed himself as close to the wall as he could. I tried to position myself as far away from both of them — without falling out of bed. In the morning the men got up first, brought me clean, if icy, water from the pump downstairs. At least I had the luxury to dress alone in a room.

We met the "invalids" as planned. Ralph had great gossip for them.

"You know what," he said, "Mohr slept with Zuck in one bed!"

NOSTALGIA FOR JUIST

Nostalgia is thinking about the past as you wish it had been, an idealized memory.

Is that how I see my school? Perhaps it really was not wonderful? I just want it to be wonderful? But why would I want that? If it had been in some way a bad experience, why would I want to cover it up? After all, I don't have to talk or write about that school. I can skip that part of my life. Everybody goes to school — nothing special about that. But I genuinely do not remember anything negative about that experience, nor anything bad happening to me there. Of course I might have suppressed the bad things, maybe some truth serum might bring it out. I don't believe that for a minute! Certainly there must have been times when we bitched about something. I would like to come up with just one incident — and I am trying — but I can't. If I ever did feel bad it was because I got a bad mark on a paper or had a fight with Hans, my classmate and boyfriend. We played hockey together, sang in the choir together and were closer for the last two years in Juist. He was a good-looking guy with blond hair worn rather long, which I liked. In the summer we would walk into the dunes in the evening to our special little valley, protected from the wind and curious eyes, an ideal spot to kiss and make out. In the winter Hans came up to my room until 9 p.m. After that no boy was allowed in a girl's room. It was not ideal. While everyone knocked on your door before they entered — the "before" was knocking with one hand and at the same time opening the door with the other. During our long vacations we stayed in close contact through daily letters. He lived in Stuttgart, a town in the south of Germany. After graduation we corresponded for a short time. And then slowly the friendship dissolved. It was 1933 and Hitler had just come to power, which hastened the end.

My friend Hilde had come to Juist later than I, and she attended the school only for the last two years. She also came from Berlin, so I had been asked to contact her during my vacation to make her familiar with life in the school. We clicked immediately and became close friends. After our graduation we stayed close until she moved out of Berlin and I had to emigrate. We found each other again after the war. She was living in Munich and I in New York. We were both married and had children. She four and I one. We managed to see each other at least once every year. Either she came to New York or I went to Munich or we met in Paris or Rome for a week. When our husbands started ailing we spent our summer vacations together in a spa in Germany. She died in 1990 of a heart attack. I still miss her.

I think the six years I spent in Juist were of major importance to me, not only for my formal education but mainly for my future *"Weltanschauung,"* world view. We learned tolerance by osmosis. The word was never mentioned. It entered my vocabulary for the first time in the U.S. There were no cliques. You were just closer with some than with others. There was a strong feeling of community. We were a closed community and had nothing to do with the people in the village. The downside was that we became snobbish. We looked down on people who went to a regular school. We felt superior just for being in the "Schule am Meer." It had nothing to do with our formal education. In fact, sometimes I thought we learned less than students in a regular high school.

But I did learn a lot about Shakespeare. A year after my arrival in Juist a big music hall was built. Our director, Luserke, was a great admirer of Shakespeare and needed a stage to produce not only Shakespeare but also short plays that he and others had written. The building was called Music Hall because all musical events would be performed in this new building, including our pre-breakfast Fugue and Prelude by Bach. We could now sit for this performance.

Lu staged "The Merchant of Venice" and "As You Like It" in German. Shaw and Wilde were presented in English. Aeschlimiss, our English teacher was in charge of those. I had a role in all of them.

My love for music was born in Juist. To this day Bach is my favorite composer. In later years, after the war when I visited Munich, Hilde always had two tickets for a Bach concert. We would both wallow in the music with teary eyes, especially when we heard the Italian Concerto, which Zuck had played on the evening we graduated.

Yes, I am nostalgic about this school but wishful thinking has nothing to do with it. It was a special and unique life we led on Juist — I was lucky to be part of it.

CAPER 1989

It was 2:45 p.m. Hilde and I were sitting in the lobby of our hotel in Bad Reichenhall. We were waiting for Ullrich and Herta. We had gone to the school in Juist together fifty years ago. Hilde, now living in Munich, had arranged this meeting as a surprise for me. I looked forward to it with mixed feelings. Particularly about Herta. I had never been close to her in school. She was not a student, she was a young teacher and only taught the lowest class (eleven year olds). But mostly she was the right hand of the director, Lu. In fact, it was rumored that she was more than his right hand. She looked very German with her long blond hair and slim figure. We sometimes called her "die Eiserne," woman of iron. She would and could handle any task no matter how difficult. I could not understand why Hilde had asked her to come because I had hardly any contact with her in school. (I found out later that it had been Ullrich's idea.)

Ullrich had been my boyfriend for a short time in school. He was also blond; I liked blond men. He was low key and easy to get along with. Preparing for this reunion, the only thing I remembered from our relationship was how once I had been so mad at him I threw a pretty vase out of my window, which crash landed in front of him. Now, facing the entrance door of the hotel, it all came back to me. I was mad at him because he was one of the boys who had sabotaged our great prank, a caper to end all capers.

I mentioned the vase incident to Hilde.

"It must have been before my time," she said. "What did he do?"

"One day Anne and I decided that we had enough of the pomades, hair lotions and particularly the hair nets the boys frequently wore. They wore them on the way to the dining room and just took them off with one sweep of the hand before they entered. They wore them on the way to class and some even kept them on when we played hockey on the beach. The boys were more concerned about their appearance, at least as far as their hair was concerned, than the girls. Anne and I had an absolutely marvelous idea. To implement it we had to wait for a full moon and we did. On that evening during dinner she and I raced through the rooms of the major culprits and raided their closets, threw all the bottles, tubes, jars and hairnets into a big laundry bag and hid it in our room. After dinner with the help of two younger girls we sat on our beds and tied pieces of string around each item of the loot. Then we tied each bottle, jar, tube and hairnet to a long clothesline, which Anne and I had lifted from the laundry. We sacrificed one of our snow-white towels and in big black letters wrote "Nimm Wasser and Seife lass Tinkturchen beiseite." (Use water and soap instead of this stuff.) We attached the towel in the middle of the clothesline. Then we waited until everybody was in bed and all the lights were out. By the light of the moon we knotted one end of the rope to our window frame on the second floor and slowly let the now heavy rope slide to the ground. Then we pulled it across the fifty meter wide yard to the opposite one story laundry building. We climbed to the roof of that building from the inside and pulled the heavy rope up to that window and tied it to the window frame. It took us a long time to accomplish the job. Crossing the yard back to our room we proudly looked at our deed. The white towel was precariously flapping in the breeze. We were ecstatic. In the morning everybody on the way to the dining room for breakfast would see it. Nobody ever missed breakfast.

"So what happened?" Hilde asked.

"What happened was, in the morning when we looked out the window the line was cut. On each roof hung a piece of floppy rope. The towel lay flat on one of them and all the bottles, hairnets, etc. were gone. We were devastated and close to tears. Everybody was talking about it and the boys were reveling in their triumph. They told us proudly that one guy had gotten up during the night, seen the line, awakened some of his friends, among them Ullrich, and they proceeded to destroy our masterpiece.

"And that's what got you so mad you smashed your pretty vase?"

"No, that's not all that happened! When we left the dining room after breakfast a big surprise was waiting for Anne and me. Our un-made beds, the bookshelves with the books intact in them, our desks and chairs were standing on the roof of the building next to ours. The white bed sheets were flapping in the wind, the blankets were half on the roof and half on the beds. Everybody saw that! Our room was bare. Not a pencil or piece of paper left. They even took the pictures off the wall. Everybody was pointing at the roof and laughing while we stood there mesmerized, fighting tears. There was no way that we could carry the furniture back. Luckily, Lu the director, saw what had happened and realized our dilemma. He told the boys to bring everything back to our room. And that was the end of the caper to end all capers.

"You never told me that story," Hilde said, and with her elbow in my ribs, whispered, "Here they come."

I looked up and thought, "Oh my god, do I look that old too?"

Herta was just as slim as I remembered, only her hair was white. She still did not wear any make-up and you could see the wrinkles in her face. It looked as if she wore the same plain clothes she had worn in Juist. Ullrich was more grey than white and had gained some weight but his face had not changed much. He was friendly and warm when he greeted me. I actually felt comfortable with him. Herta however, while she looked familiar, I did not feel comfortable with — her greeting was formal and so was mine.

Recovering from the shock of recognition, we proceeded to the terrace for coffee and cake. After the usual small talk I finally asked Ullrich:

"What did you do during the war?" I felt I had to clear the air first.

"I am an engineer. I worked behind the lines."

"Lucky you! My parents and brother were killed by Nazis." I had to get it out of my system. Ullrich was sympathetic. He elaborated on the horrors of that time.

Herta said: "I really was not aware of the persecution of Jews. It must have been terrible but it was not easy for us either."

"I believe it," I said.

"We had to run away from the Russians," Herta went on, "I sometimes did not know where my husband was."

"But he came back after the war, right?"

"Yes, he was wounded, but he is okay now."

"Lucky you," I said, again.

"But we did go through some really bad times."

At that point I could hardly wait for the check to arrive. Hilde sensed it and called the waiter. We paid and I stood up. And they left.

"I never want to see them again!" I said. "He was okay but boring. She was a Nazi! Why the hell did she want to see me?"

Hilde put her arm around me and just said "Shit!" Precisely my feelings.

ABITUR (GRADUATION) 1933

We were almost ready to graduate. The written exams were behind us. The orals were the last hurdle. The ten days between the two we studied as never before. We had little time to think about the future. For me it felt as if there was nothing after Juist. I had been in this school for six years. How would I live without it?

The day before the orals, the entire class, all ten of us (seven boys and three girls) picked up the commissioner of education from the boat, or rather the little train that got him from the boat to the island. From there we escorted him to the school a half hour walk through the dunes. Everyone tried to talk to him. I lagged behind. I was afraid of him. We did not know what subjects we would be tested in, so we had to be prepared for all of them. I was as prepared as I would ever be, and I was scared. I hoped to be tested in Physics. Dr. Dietrich had studied with me. He was one of the most popular teachers. We all watched over him when we went swimming in the ocean. He was so nearsighted that he could not see the dunes. One of us would take his hand and walk him to the beach and help him find his glasses.

Dr. Dietrich had practiced the workings of the telephone with me. He theorized that the commissioner would be impressed if a girl could explain the intricacies of this complicated mechanism. I needed something to impress that man. I was not on top of the class, but I knew that the school was eager to pass us all. Their reputation depended on it. I did not sleep well that night.

In the morning the ten of us were herded into Tante Mia's living room. She was in charge of the housekeeping and the kitchen. We spent the time between the tests in her apartment. She served us tea and cookies.

The first subject that I was called in for was English. The usually familiar music hall with its grand piano and harpsichord, chairs set in a half circle around the instruments, was now just one big hall. Everything was squeezed into one corner. It looked cold and unfamiliar. Against one wall was a long table. All our teachers sat behind it, including the commissioner of education who sat in the middle, flanked by Lu and our English teacher Aeschlimiss. Her husband, next to her, wore a big black bow around his neck instead of a tie. Our director sat on the other side of the commissioner. And there was Zuckmayer, called Zuck, our music teacher. He had a famous brother, a playwright Carl Zuckmayer. We often wondered how he felt sitting on this little island teaching music while his famous brother was celebrated all over Germany. And there was Dr. Dietrich in his good blue suit and a new tie. They were all there, even those who did not teach the upper classes. Mr. Hafner our art teacher and the custodian of the little aquarium he had built, looked like Santa Claus with his long grayish beard.

As I walked to the little table opposite them, all eyes were on me. Aeschlimiss stood up and handed me a book with shaking hands. Pointing to a paragraph she said, "Fraulein Berger, please read this and translate it into German."

"Fraulein Berger," I thought. Herr Stolz, Fraulein Mueseler, nobody was ever addressed like that. I hardly knew she was talking to me. But I did as I was told.

"Good," Aeschlimiss said, and I was dismissed.

Back to Tante Mia's living room and her tea and cookies.

The next subject was German. Lu himself taught German to the two upper classes. However we had actually studied German literature only in the last year. The year before it was all Shakespeare. Because he was an ardent admirer of Shakespeare, we studied Shakespeare in the German literature class. He even brought Prof. Hecht, a famous Shakespearian scholar from Heidelberg, to talk to us. Among other things Professor Hecht told us that the Schlegel and Tiek translation was better that the original!

Now, with the Commissioner present, Lu covered the material of the last year, German literature. Everything went well until he asked me, "Which play is most characteristic of the Sturm and Drang period?" Goethe's and Schiller's plays went through my head but I did not know which one was most characteristic of this particular period. Suddenly Zuck got up, walked slowly behind the row of examiners holding his fisted hand straight up, stopping behind the Commissioner. He looked at me "Goetz von Berliching," I said. (The hero of this play had an iron fist, which made it famous.) Zuck smiled and I kept a straight face.

"Good," said Lu, "thank you Fraulein Berger." Back to Tante Mia and tea and cookies.

After lunch the exams were moved to the physics and chemistry rooms. I was the second person to be called in. Dr. Dietrich smiled at me through his thick glasses and asked me to explain the workings of the telephone. I wanted to smile too but I did not dare. I went to the big switchboard and started plugging the pegs into the holes explaining what I was doing and why I was doing it. Then the Commissioner asked me a theoretical question, which I proudly answered.

"Thank you, Fraulein Berger," he said.

Again, a return to Tante Mia's tea and cookies.

Aeschlimiss came in to call Hilde for her math test.

"You were very impressive at that switchboard," she said. "You are finished."

"Is that a good or a bad sign?"

"I cannot answer that," she said and walked out the door with Hilde.

More tea and cookies.

This is my last day of school. No more walks on the beach, no more hockey playing on the beach. No more swims before breakfast, no more Bach before breakfast.

Tante Mia interrupted my thoughts, offering more cookies and tea.

Finally we were all dismissed. Nobody said a word. We were each in our private world — waiting. Tante Mia was as tense as we were, running around with her cookie tray. I did not want any more cookies. I wanted to agonize about leaving Juist. I had never been homesick in all these years but now I was afraid I would be homesick for the school, for Lu's personal wake-up call, the ocean, the breezes, running into Hilde's room at 10 p.m. to schmooze, or walking with her across the yard to the bathroom.

Suddenly Zuck stormed in. We were terrified. But he was smiling as he grabbed some cookies and said, "You all passed! But please make a serious face when you come in."

We walked in a funeral march step back to the music hall. All the teachers were sitting again at the long table against the wall. The ten of us lined up in front of them like soldiers. Their faces were serious and so were ours. Hilde pushed her elbow into my side. We were on the brink of giddiness. After a few seconds the Commissioner stood up, "Congratulations, you all passed," he said and proceeded to make a little speech to which nobody listened. We just stood there looking at him. When the handshaking began the tension was broken. We started laughing and congratulating each other.

"I have to call my parents," someone yelled and started running to the one and only telephone in the office. We all ran after him and stood in line to call our families. Zuck came with us. He winked at me and I embraced him and whispered, "Thank you."

Then he asked us all, "What shall I play for you tonight?"

"The Italian Concerto," we replied.

After dinner the entire school, including the Commissioner sat in the once again familiar looking music hall, listening to Bach's beautiful piece. Zuck played it on the harpsichord. It sounded more beautiful than ever.

The next day all ten of us escorted the Commissioner back to the little train that would bring him to the boat. This time I did not lag behind.

MY JOB IN BERLIN 1933

I had graduated from high school. After six years away from home — in my boarding school on the little island in the North Sea — I was back in Berlin for good. It was 1933. Jews were not allowed to go to college anymore. My father offered me a job in his tie manufacturing business, which I gladly accepted. I worked in the office with three other women and was treated like any other employee — with one exception. When my father came back from lunch, which he had in the same restaurant with the same people every day, he would lie down for a short nap. Then he would call a young girl, the same one every day, to make coffee for him. When the coffee was ready he would call me into his office and we would share fifteen minutes over coffee and zwieback.

One day someone came into our office while we were eating our brown-bagged lunch and said: "Everybody has to go to Ms. Wohl's office. Take your handbag and keys along."

"Do you know what is going on?" my colleagues asked me.

"I have no idea." We grabbed our things and joined the line in front of Ms. Wohl's office. Nobody knew what was going on. Someone tried the door to the staircase. It was locked. One of the maintenance men was guarding it.

"You don't have to try the other doors; they are all locked too. Orders from the boss."

The line moved very slowly. My father called one person in at a time. Ms. Wohl was my father's right hand. A middle age plus woman, she had been with the company over twenty years and was the only one who had her own office other than my father. She was respected but also feared. Whenever someone came out of her office now we would ask: "What happened?"

"They looked at my cash with a magnifying glass, glanced at my keys and gave it all back to me."

"What are they looking for?"

"I don't know, they don't say a word."

I couldn't figure it out either. I was wondering how long I would have to stay in line here. Now I wished I would get special treatment. I was the boss's daughter. Why didn't he send me home? I was worried I would not be able to go to my hangout, Zuntz, after work. Meanwhile the line moved at a snail's pace.

Why did I start working here? It was a temporary job as far as I was concerned. I had no intention of making this business my career. However I suspected that it was my father's dream that I would make it my future. (In 1933 nobody believed that Hitler would stay in power for long.) He moved me around. I had to work in the shipping and receiving departments and I even had to work in the cutting room. He took me on a buying trip to Crefeld where the weaving mills were. In the hotel we had two rooms next to each other. After the porter put the luggage down he whispered, "Shall I open the connecting door?"

"No thanks, he is my father!"

He introduced me to everybody and encouraged me to choose some of the patterns, which he promptly bought. In the evenings we had delicious dinners with wine.

Now I did not even have a cup of coffee, not to mention the zwieback. At last it was my turn. I put all my money and keys on the table. My father and Ms. Wohl looked at the keys and inspected each coin with a magnifying glass.

"What are you looking for?" I asked.

"For weeks somebody has been stealing money out of Ms. Wohl's purse. Her door is always locked. We are tying to find the thief."

"How?" I asked.

"Go back to your work," said my father.

If I was late to Zuntz, I had to take the bus home. It was a forty-minute walk to my house. I liked that walk, particularly if Heinz walked me home.

Suddenly everybody was sent back to work. They knew who had stolen the money.

In Germany everything less than ten marks were coins. There were one, two and five mark pieces. They knew whoever stole the money grabbed whatever she or he could get out of Ms. Wohl's purse. Ms. Wohl never knew exactly how much change she had in it. To catch the thief my father had an ingenious idea. He took fifty marks in different denominations, all coins, and with a nail put a dent into every one. That money went into Ms. Wohl's handbag. As she did every day, she left her office and locked the door. When she returned, some of the money was missing again. This time they knew exactly how much it was. The only person who had the key to the office was a woman who had worked closely with Ms. Wohl for fifteen years. She also had most of the marked money in her bag. But not all. Two other people had dented coins in their wallets too. The woman had borrowed money from those two people, and had paid them back with the stolen coins.

Ms. Wohl was very upset. My father fired the thief on the spot. He did not take any further action. He was sorry for her and felt that losing her job was enough punishment.

I was proud of him. He had handled the whole thing quietly and discreetly. I got out on time and rushed to Zuntz with a good story to tell.

ZUNTZ

I don't know how it started, but I ended up at Zuntz every afternoon. Back in Berlin after graduating from school and working in my father's business, Zuntz became my hang-out; I was addicted to it. If I had a dentist appointment after work and could not stop there it spoiled my day.

Zuntz was a one-of-a-kind café. The major attraction was the price. A cup of coffee, black, was twenty pfennig (about six cents); with milk it was twenty-five pfennig. There were two floors. The young people sat upstairs. The cake eaters downstairs. These were mostly middle-aged or older women who had been shopping in the Kadewe, a big department store. They stopped at Zuntz for their coffee and cake break.

I bought my pink coupon for black coffee, went to the second floor, handed it to the waitress, got my delicious brew, no tip, and could sit for hours. It was always crowded upstairs. When I could not find a table for myself I would ask permission to sit at one that had an empty chair. That's how I, and everyone else, made friends.

We drank our black coffee, just coffee, we never had cake, and we smoked. We did not need matches; we could always light a cigarette on someone else's. We smoked the same brand, Caid, the cheapest. Cigarettes came in different price ranges. You could tell by the package if someone smoked a cheap or expensive one. Caids even came four in a little red box for ten pfennig. I embarrassed my father once. My mother was out of town and he took me out for dinner at an elegant restaurant. When the coffee came I pulled out my little red box of Caids. He shook his head and whispered, "Put them back in your bag!"

At Zuntz, we would have been surprised if someone smoked an expensive brand — maybe even suspicious.

It was 1934. Hitler was in power. Politics were on everyone's mind. We were all on the left of the political spectrum, optimistic with reservations. We were very young. Some of us were students and some were working. Some were Jewish and some were not; it did not matter to us — then. We were all biding our time, hoping things would change and afraid they wouldn't.

One of the men, Heinz, would sometimes walk me home. It was a good half hour to my house. I had to be home at 6:30 for dinner. He and I became friends; he wanted more but I didn't. He still escorted me home and I liked that. However, I never let him bring me to the door. I always walked the last four blocks without him. I did not want anyone at Zuntz to know that I lived in a private house in Gunnewald, an elegant part of Berlin. I was afraid they would not trust me anymore and consider me an outsider. While I lived in a nice house, my personal budget was limited. In that sense I was one of them. But I knew it was not the same.

When I was back in Berlin after the war, I looked for Zuntz. It's gone. Anyway, it would not be the same. I would have to sit downstairs now.

ON THE ORIENT EXPRESS 1935

I was going to Istanbul on the Orient Express. My friend Anne from boarding school had written: "Come to Istanbul, you can stay with us. Wigand (her husband) will teach you dental technique."

It was December 1935 and I was twenty-one years old. It was my chance to get out of Germany. If I learned a trade I could work anywhere. I did not even have to know the language. I decided to go, and my father bought a ticket for the Orient Express.

Anne's father, a famous dentist, had gone to Istanbul at the invitation of the Turkish government. That invitation got him out of prison. He was politically on the far left. He left Germany immediately after his release and took his entire family along. Three children, his ex-wife, his mistress and Wigand who became Anne's husband.

And now I was standing in front of this fancy train, surrounded by my family and friends. The conductor in his snappy blue uniform matching the blue cars had brought my suitcase into my compartment. I was in a trance. It was hard to fathom that I was going to this exotic country — away from Berlin and my parents. For forty-eight hours I would be on the luxurious train with its gold letters announcing to the world on every car: "Orient Express." I was in awe and also afraid. Two days and two nights alone on this moving hotel was not something I looked forward to. I had embarked on this trip almost as a lark. I did not know how long I would or could stay. I had no goal other than the need to get out of Germany. Now I was thinking of my parents and brother

Bert standing next to me. When would I see them again? Only the parting was on my mind. I half wished I could get it over with, and then, again I hoped that we would leave late so I could stay longer.

My father reassured me again and again that he had paid for all my meals and tips on the train in advance and that everything would go smoothly. He had given me 25 marks, about thirteen dollars, the maximum amount I was allowed to take out of Germany.

"Don't spend the money on the train. Keep it for an emergency."

I could not figure out what kind of an emergency I might encounter. The "all aboard" brought me back to the moment.

"Lock the door of your compartment at night! Don't forget to send the telegram when you arrive. Write!"

I rushed into my compartment and opened the window. My face was wet from kisses and my own tears.

At first the train moved slowly, very slowly. My brother and parents were walking alongside it, Bert holding on to my hand to the end of the platform, my father and mother waving their white handkerchiefs. Then, though still slowly, the train went through Berlin, stopping at two more stations within the city. I stood at the window until the city slowly disappeared. At last, I sat down on the blue couch, watching the landscape rushing by. It must be true; I was on my way to Istanbul. There had been a big white sign on my car saying "Istanbul via Prague, Budapest, Belgrade and Sofia." These were the only further stops we would make on this long trip.

A knock on the door interrupted my thoughts.

The conductor asked me, "Can I have your passport please?"

"My passport? Why do you want my passport?"

"I'll keep it for you during the trip. Then I will not have to wake you up when we pass a border during the night."

I just stood there looking at him. He looked back at me smiling and showed me three passports he had already collected. Hesitatingly, I handed him mine and closed the door. I did not feel comfortable about this transaction.

The train consisted of three passenger cars. One each from London, Paris and Berlin. Not all the passengers were going all the way to Istanbul. Only five people were in my car.

I sat alone at a table for dinner. Next to the shining white dishes with their blue border was a lot of silver cutlery, forks, knifes and spoons. Several crystal glasses reflected the light, and fresh flowers made it all look festive. I ate everything that was offered but drank nothing but plain water. I had to save my money for emergencies. I did not talk to anybody. It was a lonely experience. But I did feel special in this luxurious atmosphere. I rushed back to my compartment. It had miraculously changed into a bedroom! When I came out of my little bathroom, which consisted of a toilet, a sink and a big bunch of snow-white towels initialed in blue, ready to go to bed, I heard a knock on my door.

"I am sorry to disturb you," the conductor said, "I think I left my key to the linen closet in your room. May I come in to look for it?"

"I don't see any key here."

"Please let me in and search for it. I need it in the morning to put clean sheets on the beds."

"It is not here! I am looking all over!"

"Are you sure?"

"Yes," I said, annoyed. "Good night."

"Good night," he answered and left. I double-checked the lock and wished I had a chair to put in front of the door — I was uncomfortable. I was depending on this man. He made up my room while I was in the dining car, he knew all the languages of the countries we passed through, he was the only person I could talk to on this long trip, but most important of all, he had my passport.

The next afternoon we arrived in Belgrade. A friend I had met the year before on a skiing trip in Yugoslavia was waiting for me on the platform. I had written to him and was not sure if he would come to meet me. We spent a pleasant hour reminiscing over coffee in the waiting room of the station. It was a welcome diversion.

After Belgrade we were three in my car. Judging by the number of diners that night, there were only ten passengers on the entire train.

One more night to go. We were supposed to arrive in Istanbul at 11 a.m. the next morning. I had no trouble falling asleep that night. A loud knock on my door woke me up. "Not again," I thought.

"What do you want?" I screamed.

"The Turkish border police are here. Your passport is not valid."

"What?"

"The Turkish border police are here. Open the door." I heard several voices and opened the door. I was in pajamas, the conductor in his elegant blue outfit and the Turk in his crumpled uniform were staring at me. I was shaking.

"The picture in your passport has no stamp on it. He will not give it back to you. You have to go to the police at the station in Istanbul to get it back," said the conductor.

I looked at the picture in my precious little brown book. It was true, there was no stamp on it. Anybody could replace it with another photo.

"Okay," I said, closed the door and sat down. What if they don't give it back to me? I wondered. And if they do what am I going to do with an invalid passport? Stay in Turkey forever?

I got dressed, went for breakfast, hoping Anne and Wigand would find a solution. I could hardly wait to get off the train now.

I started walking back and forth in my car looking at the snow covered Turkish landscape. Suddenly the train stopped. It just stood there in the middle of nowhere. Were we stuck in the snow? I started talking to the couple in my car. Strange how an emergency overcomes shyness immediately.

We cornered the conductor. "Why aren't we moving?"

"In Turkey the Orient Express runs on one track. We have to wait for the opposite train to pass us."

To top it off it started to snow again. Maybe the opposite train is stuck in the snow? The Orient Express on one track? What kind of country am I going to? We might have to stay here until spring when the snow melted — without food or water. Anything seems to be possible here. And I don't even have a valid passport — in fact I have no passport. I can't even prove who I am. The train did not move. One hour passed — two hours passed. The car got colder and it was still snowing. Maybe we would stay here forever?

Four hours! What if Anne can't wait for me at the station? Will I be able to get a taxi and pay with my 25 mark emergency money? And how will I communicate with them? What if the police decided not to give me back my passport? Instead they might keep me too! Anne has no telephone. I can't even let her know where I might land. Five hours! If I do get a taxi maybe my school French will help. Of course, a taxi might drive a single woman straight into a harem. I am slowly losing my mind.

Six hours — we are moving. A train from the opposite direction is passing us. We arrive in snowy Istanbul six hours late. Anne was standing on the platform shivering. I was never so happy to see her. We immediately went to the police station. I got my passport back. They told me to go to the German Consulate to have it stamped. I was not eager to go there but I had to, and the next day they did stamp my picture. I had no problem.

ISTANBUL 1936

From the station we took a taxi to Anne's apartment, a luxury neither of us could afford. However I considered it an emergency and paid Anne back from my 25 mark "emergency money." When we arrived at her address she had to ring for the concierge to open the door. No tenant had the key to the building. He had to be on call day and night. Later when I acquired a boyfriend, it was embarrassing to get the poor man out of bed in the middle of the night. I wondered what he would have thought if I came home with a different one every night.

Our living quarters were rather limited. The apartment was on the main floor. At least the entrance door was on the main floor; actually it was a half story below street level. There was a living room to the left and to the right a little hall, the end of which was Wigand's laboratory. I was supposed to learn his trade — dental technician — in Istanbul. The theory was: whatever you can do with your hands can support you in any country. You did not have to know the language. Nobody mentioned that you also needed some finger dexterity for that kind of work, which was utterly lacking in my case.

Wigand and Anne slept in an alcove opposite the entrance door. Privacy was established for these relative newlyweds by a rather flimsy curtain. My sleeping area was along the little hall between the alcove and the kitchen. It was a tiny room open to the hall. Without a curtain. It contained a bed, a chair and a small table. In order for any one to go to the bathroom or the dental lab, he had to pass my little space. At least, we did have a full bathroom with a regular door. The arrangement was rather cozy. Whenever I wanted to get dressed or undressed I would announce my intention so Wigand would not happen to pass my quarters. At first I was uncomfortable. Did these friends really want me to come, I wondered. I felt like an intruder. But that lasted only a few days. I quickly felt at home and became part of the family.

There were a few rules I had to learn: "You *never* run on the street, not to catch a streetcar nor for any other reason and you always carry a pin with you."

"A pin?"

"When you get on a crowded streetcar someone will most likely pinch you in the behind. Don't get upset about it, you will get used to it, it is up to you then to retaliate with the pin."

"Anything else?"

"Never walk alone on the street after dark, never!"

The first day I went marketing with Anne to get a sense of the city. Minarets covered the sky. Lattices braced some of the windows behind which the women used to sit and look out into the street, and some women still sat behind these guards. Occasionally we could see a little piece of their garments. On the famous bridge over the Bosporus automobiles, camels, horse drawn carts and streetcars all fought for space. It was noisy but somehow it was a peaceful noise.

This was my first experience with a non-western country. People were dressed differently, particularly the women. Many of them covered their faces and were dressed all in black. Some of the men looked Western in their business suits, but workers and peasants wore the wide Turkish pants and red fezzes. Some carried heavy loads of fruit or vegetables colorfully arranged in big baskets on their backs. They called out the prices while they walked. You had to flag them down like a taxi and bargain. You could always chisel them down a few cents; it was part of the game. Gypsy women nursing their babies sat on the street begging. Most of the babies looked old enough to go to school. Little children dressed in rags were running around day and night. It made for a vivid, lively picture and I liked it.

Later when I was not "working," I would go with Anne on her errands. I preferred that to sitting in the lab chiseling away on my giant plaster tooth. The first assignment Wigand had given me was to make a molar out of a five-centimeter block of plaster. It was not the most fascinating thing I'd ever done, so whenever possible I left with Anne to buy chopped meat and salad. Our daily dinner always consisted of hamburgers, fried potatoes and green salad. For dessert we had coffee and cookies. We could not afford anything fancier. What we could afford was Turkish coffee. At night the three of us would sometimes sit in one of the many little coffee houses and drink their delicious brew. The cups were so small that there was hardly more than one sip but it was luscious and sweet. Turkish coffee is boiled with sugar; it is not like espresso but just as strong. Only men would sit in these coffee houses, Turkish women did not go out at night, not with their men or without them. The men would talk and smoke their water pipes. Sometimes more than one person was connected to a pipe.

Heinz, a friend of Wigand and Anne, frequently joined us in these outings and I began to enjoy his company. Eventually the two of us would go out alone on weekends. He was part of a small group of Germans who had fled Hitler's regime for Turkey. When my conscience bothered me I would sit in the lab and work on the plaster. But I did not enjoy it and tried to get away whenever possible. The lab had a window to a little court populated with cats of all stripes and colors. At least twenty would peacefully walk around looking for food. Cats and rats were in abundance in Istanbul. One night on the way to a movie we saw a couple of giant rats chased out of a building as everyone watched them cross the street and enter another building. That was also the evening when I tested walking alone at night. I had started to amble about ten yards in front of my friends. Two men came towards me with their arms stretched out. I kept on walking and so did they, never taking their arms down. At the last second I turned around and ran back to my protectors. The men's arms were aimed straight at my breasts.

After the experience with the rats I was glad that we had all the cats in our little court, it made me feel kind of secure. Sometimes a few would jump into the lab snooping around. We usually just chased them out. However, one morning Wigand just about had it with them. He climbed out the window with a little bottle of ether and sprayed it into every cat's rear end, hoping they would disappear. They didn't. Instead they all just held their tails straight up and meowed a little louder. The court looked like a forest of tails. It was cruel but funny. The next day they were all back to normal.

Since Wigand was the breadwinner, Anne and I were not only responsible for our delicious food but we also had to make deliveries to dentists. Eventually, I found my way around the city alone, got used to being pinched on the streetcar but never dared to use my pin. One of Wigand's customers was a deaf and dumb dentist. He had learned to lip read and speak in Berlin. The first time I went into his office I spoke to him in French. Whereupon he said; "You can speak German, I understand it." He and his wife frequently came to visit us to share our cookies and coffee. He followed the conversation like a hearing person only his speech was different. He was a most amazing man, he spoke four languages "only in English I have a bad accent," he said.

One afternoon I came home from an errand and found Anne sitting in the steaming bathtub. The bathroom door was wide open.

"What are you doing in the bathtub?"

"I am trying to get my period. I am a week late."

"Did you try jumping off a table?" She had not but was willing to give it a chance.

"Maybe we could put my table on top of yours, that might work better."

"Good idea, Ruth," said Wigand and we both laughed hysterically. Anne did not laugh, she opened the faucet to add more hot water. In the end she did not jump off any table and she was not pregnant either.

It became obvious to me that I would not learn dental technique at the pace I was going. My stay in Istanbul was more of a vacation and I enjoyed it but what about my future? I could not stay with them forever — doing practically nothing. My father did send me 25 marks every month, the limit the Germans permitted to be mailed to a foreign country. I gave 15 marks to Anne every month and kept the rest, which barely covered my carfares and the occasional coffee. And what if Anne had been pregnant? They would have needed my little room for the baby. It was obvious to me that I could not stay much longer. But I did not know what to do about it. Then my parents came to the rescue.

I received a letter from my mother, which said in part: "If you want to come back to Berlin, you are not allowed by law to stay longer than three months in Istanbul." It came just at the right time. By now I had been in Turkey for two months and I knew I could not stay forever. Besides, Anne and Wigand had started making plans for their future; they were contemplating going to Palestine. I certainly could not tag along. Besides, chiseling away on my plaster molars and running errands had lost their attraction. Going home was no goal but it would get me out of the dead end I felt I was in. Berlin would mean starting from scratch or maybe I could learn mechanical dentistry in earnest if I put my mind to it. I decided to go back. The decision itself made me feel better.

It was not that I wasn't having a good time, particularly since I had acquired a boyfriend, Heinz, who had taken me sightseeing to the famous mosques, palaces and on an unforgettable rowing expedition on the Bosporus. There we came to a small bridge, which was lined with little boys. Heinz told me, "Watch out, they will pee on us."

I looked up, and sure enough, the little fellows opened their flies and peed nice little arcs straight at the boat. Luckily the bridge was too high and they missed us. But it was a strange sight!

Heinz had also tried valiantly to take me to a Turkish restaurant, but we had to turn around immediately. The smell of lamb was unbearable to me. We settled for good coffee and very sweet cake. Now I asked him to go with me to the Bazaar. I had saved a little money for emergencies again, what emergencies I had no idea, but somehow one always had to save money for emergencies. So I thought it a good idea to spend it now on gifts.

The Bazaar with its open stalls and little shops, what a sight. The shining brass and copper wares, large and small trays, brightly colored rugs hanging outside the stalls, jewelry shops with mostly antique silver, or so they said. Men stood around, trying to get us interested in their precious goods. Heinz was an expert in handling them, he just nodded his head and said, "Yok," which means anything negative like, "no," "don't want it," or "leave me alone."

We ended up in a nice little store where he knew the owner who greeted us both like old friends and who spoke French. He immediately called for coffee. A little boy came with the delicious brew, balancing the cups on a brass scale, two round trays on each side held the cups. As soon as we finished, he ordered more coffee. It was like a social visit, the men making conversation about business and the weather, and the storeowner asking me how I liked Istanbul. Very slowly we eased into the purpose of our visit. We asked to see some stones. He opened his treasure box and a piece of black velvet a mosaic of stones in all colors and sizes sparkled in the bright lamplight. Since my fortune was limited I picked up a little moonstone and tried to find a matching one. (I was thinking of cufflinks.)

"Are you looking for three more?" asked the merchant.

I was and could not understand how he had known it. Heinz just shrugged his shoulders and did not seem surprised. In no time we had four matching stones. Then, however, I discovered an old silver bracelet for which I got a real hankering but could hardly afford. Heinz offered to buy it for me if he could get it for the right price. The fun began. We had done a little bargaining with the stones and probably paid too much but they were not expensive. The bracelet was in a different league.

"How much?" Heinz started.

"This is a very special piece, it's an antique, look at the craftsmanship, your friend has excellent taste."

"How much?" He gave the price. Heinz nodded his head "yok." The owner went down a little. "Yok." Heinz pulled me out of the little store. I was sad, I liked the bracelet, but bargaining is bargaining. He knew what he was doing. We were hardly fifteen meters away when he came running after us, lured us back into the store with fresh coffee and the bargaining started for real. I just sat there and listened as the numbers went back and forth. It was like a tennis tournament and these two players masters at the game. Heinz was waiting for the magic number, which finally was mentioned and he bought the bracelet. I was happy but he still had doubts: "It was too easy, I probably paid too much." I still have the bracelet.

While I was busy shopping, my parents had mailed me my train ticket. It was not the Orient Express this time. I was going third class all the way. Anne made sandwiches for me and I had a little money to buy something to drink or eat at the stations. I certainly could not afford to go to the dining car. Anne and Heinz brought me to the station. We were in a somber mood. "When, or if, will we meet again" was on everyone's mind. We silently embraced, and I climbed on the train.

It was crowded, and we were eight people in the compartment. None of the others were going all the way to Berlin. All of them were loaded down with suitcases, packages and boxes. One party had a huge bottle of wine. None of them spoke a language I understood and nobody understood me. But they talked to me anyway and I to them, using hands and feet to explain something, without much success, except that we laughed a lot. It was rather a humorous situation. Suddenly the big bottle was opened. I had a flashback: Heinz and I were on the Black Sea and a Turkish couple offered us something to eat. I made a face but Heinz whispered, "It is a big insult to refuse food or drink!" so I ate it then. Now I took the cup that was handed to me and drank whatever was in there, considered myself lucky to be handed it first.

The train kept on rolling and soon we would be in Sofia, where I had a three-hour layover. The conductor came in and spoke to me in German, pointed to the single young man in the compartment who had smiled at me frequently and who was smiling at me now. "He is getting off in Sofia, he wants to show you the city while you are here. He will bring you back to the train on time." The young man looked at me with great anticipation and I smiled at him and got off with him at Sofia.

He took me on a horse and buggy ride through the city. All I remember is that I saw the big palace and that I looked at my watch every five minutes. Whatever he was saying to me I couldn't understand. But I didn't care. I had a nice side trip and could now brag that I had been in Bulgaria too. How I had the nerve to go with this strange man on a ride in a totally foreign city in a country where I could not understand a word, I don't know to this day.

The compartment became empty after we left the Balkans. I had one entire bench for myself the second night and could stretch out and sleep a little. I arrived in Berlin hungry, tired and dirty and glad to see my parents at the station. I think they were relieved to see me too.

ERNST 1937

Ernst entered my life after I came back from Istanbul. He was a friend of my cousin Walter who lived in Berlin and was our dinner guest every Sunday noon. Ernst came to pick Walter up one Sunday afternoon. They asked me to join them for a movie and supper. Ernst was a good-looking man despite his slightly thinning blond hair. He had blue eyes and wore glasses. I liked his looks and accepted the invitation. (In hindsight I am not sure if Walter intended to make a match.) I was twenty-three years old and Ernst was ten years older. He and his younger brother Kurt owned a men's clothing factory. They shared a big apartment with their mother who was divorced from their father.

Ernst called me the following Tuesday and asked me out for Saturday night. I accepted gladly. We saw each other again the next weekend. Saturday nights together soon became the rule.

He took me to elegant places for dinner and dancing, places I had never been to before. (In 1937 Jews could still go out freely in Berlin.) The women in these restaurants were all elegantly dressed. I felt a little underdressed in my best wool suit and silk blouse. I did not own a fancy dress. Ernst did not seem to mind. We were happily eating and waltzing along. He was an excellent dancer. I particularly liked to dance the Tango with him; he taught me some intricate steps and told me always to look in the direction we moved. Sometimes he kissed my hand after a dance. I liked that.

While I was comfortable enough in my suit and silk blouse, I still pestered my mother to buy me a more appropriate dress. I wanted to look as attractive as I possibly could. I not only liked

Ernst, I seemed to be falling in love with him. I began to look forward to our always too short taxi rides home. It was on one of these rides that we kissed for the first time.

I don't know if it was the cuddling or the new black dress I finally got, but we began to see each other not only on Saturdays but also for walks on Sundays and occasionally I picked him up at his office and we'd spend the rest of the day together.

And one day, he invited me for dinner at his house. He wanted me to meet Kurt and his mother. I was a little apprehensive. I arrived punctually, if nervously, with a bunch of flowers for the hostess. I liked Kurt. He was cordial and able to break the ice with some jokes. (When I got to know Kurt better I realized that jokes were part of his survival kit.) I can't say that I liked their mother. After she put a piece of chicken breast on Kurt's plate, a leg on Ernst's and a wing on mine, Ernst protested and a piece of breast was added to the wing. I was embarrassed and felt very uncomfortable.

On the way home, Ernst tried to console me. "Don't take it seriously; she is more than a little crazy."

"I hope she does not invite me again because I won't come."

"Don't worry about it — she won't. I invited you to this dinner. Besides she does not like any woman Kurt or I go out with."

In a strange way this incident made us feel closer. A few days later we decided to go on a skiing trip for a week. I was delighted! The only problem was how to break that news to my parents. I told my mother the truth and for my father invented a group I was joining. It worked!

It was a perfect week; even the weather was cooperative. We skied all day in the sun and had dinner in the cozy little hotel every night. I was relaxed and felt secure and protected.

It was on one of these cozy evenings that Ernst started talking about leaving Germany with Kurt and his mother. "After I sell our business we will go to Holland and from there to America."

Before I realized what his leaving would mean to me, he looked at me and added "Will you join me in Amsterdam once we are safely there?"

I embraced and kissed him and promised I would. (While I also had thought about leaving Germany - every Jewish person did - I had no idea how to go about it.)

"But why do you have to go to Holland first?"

"I have a cousin in Amsterdam who has the money I was able to smuggle out of the country. You know now we cannot take more than ten marks out legally." (Ten marks at that time was about five dollars.)

"I did not know that."

"We will have to live on that money until we start working in America."

I was quiet. Suddenly my future was written out for me. Not only would I be with Ernst but I also would get out of Germany. What would my parents say? I did not want to think about my parents. I wanted to wallow in my happy thoughts. And I did until Ernst put his arm around me, took my hand and silently pulled me up the stairs to our room.

ERNST'S EXIT 1938

I was sitting at the window waiting for the mailman. I was waiting for a letter from Ernst — postmarked in Holland. "I'll send you a wire as soon as we are across the border and confirm it with a letter," he had said. I had received the telegram but no letter.

Six days before, his mother and I stood in front of the Alexanderplatz Prison at 8 a.m. sharp to pick up Ernst and his brother Kurt. We were not sure if they would be released that day. Mr. G. the man in charge of visitations had given me a hint that they would come out after eight weeks — at least I thought he had given me a hint — I was not sure. I was smoking non-stop walking back and forth in front of the big prison door. "What if they don't come out? What am I going to do then? Will we wait here all day?"

And then finally about 9:30 a.m. they appeared. They were walking slowly each carrying a paper bag with their meager belongings. I was running towards them with tears in my eyes. They had been in "protective custody" a euphemism for prison.

Two men in civilian clothes had come to their office, in the middle of the afternoon. "Leave everything and come with us," was all they said after identifying themselves. I witnessed this scene. We all knew what it meant. It was the second time. The first time they were released after eight days. The men rose. Ernst pulled his little black address book out and carefully hid it under the chair pillow. From the corner of his eyes he looked at me. I stayed behind briefly, picked up the little black book and then caught up with them. I took Ernst's hand and silently walked along. When they entered the ugly red building on Alexanderplatz, I kissed him and left. I did not turn around.

"When will they come out this time? And what am I going to do now?" I wondered looking at the mailman who passed us by once again.

I knew very well what I had to do then. A few days later I went into that big ugly building on Alexanderplatz where I was referred to Mr. G. who was in charge of prisoner's visitations. Mr. G. greeted me with "Heil Hitler" and a big smile.

I whispered "good morning," and smiled back. "I would like to visit Ernst Larson."

"You can visit him once a week."

"Can I bring him something?"

"Just clean underwear and before each visit you need a pass from me. You can visit him today. Here is your pass." And then he told me where the visiting room was.

Across a two-meter long table I could see Ernst once a week. I shoved the clean underwear across that table. "How are you?"

"Fine." He did not look fine. It was obvious he had not shaved in a couple of days. He stroked his face with both hands. "I hope they will give me a shave today. But I don't know."

"Maybe when I come next week you'll get it just in time for my visit." What a stupid thing to say, what difference does it make?

"Thanks for coming and keep on writing. It's the only thing to look forward to here."

"I will. See you next week."

Through the lawyer, we found out that the brothers had to sell their business immediately. They manufactured men's clothing. Kurt took care of the factory. Ernst was in charge of buying, the salesmen and the administration. It was a good business. Now they were forced to sell it while in prison. Mr. G. permitted me to attend that meeting. I sat next to Ernst and sneaked cigarettes and matches into his pocket. I even got to kiss him good-bye.

The following week after his usual "Heil Hitler," Mr. G. waved his finger half threatening and half joking at me. "Fraulein Berger, matches! How could you give him matches? Do you know how dangerous that is? I really have to take all privileges away from you."

My head went down. I was afraid to look at him. I was fighting tears.

"However, I will make an exception. You can go and visit him today, but no more letters."

"Thank you, Mr. G. When will they come out?"

"How long were they in the first time?"

"Eight days."

"I guess that will be weeks."

"You mean they come out after eight weeks?"

"No, I really don't know when they will come out." (That was the hint.)

From prison, Ernst, Kurt, their mother and I went to my parents' house where a sumptuous lunch was waiting: cheese, eggs, herring, cold cuts, fresh rolls and coffee. All anybody touched was the coffee.

"You can't go back to your apartment. You have to stay in our house. They might come and pick you up again," I said.

It was a chancy suggestion. Mr. G. knew my address. My gut feeling was that he would not betray us. In a crazy way I trusted this man. He did let me know when they would be released. Walter, a friend, spent the night in their apartment. The next day at noon we met Walter in Café Unter Den Linden. "The police called last night. You have to leave!"

Suitcases were packed. Kurt picked up the car they had bought several months ago. They intended to transform it into cash once they were in Holland. Ernst emptied his bank account and put the money into his shoes. None of the three had a passport!

The goal was Aachen. A German city bordering on Belgium and Holland. I rode with them to the last subway station.

When the mailman passed my house again on the fourth day, I decided to take the night train to Aachen, an eight-hour ride from Berlin. My aunt and her family lived there. The train was very crowded. I sat on my suitcase in the third class corridor all night — worrying. Were all these people going to Aachen to sneak across the border? What if some SS man decided to ask everyone why they are on this train? "To visit my aunt," I had that figured that out.

My cousin Heinz picked me up from the train. We went straight to the Hotel Adler, the center of illegal border crossings and a supermarket for false identity papers. Heinz knew his way around. We went into the hotel's big restaurant. It was filled to capacity. He asked Mr. Adler if he had seen Ernst.

"All three are here, and their father is here too."

"I'll meet them at 2 p.m. at the train station," their father told me. "They ran out of money; that's why they called for me. Why don't you come to the station too?"

"I will."

At 2 p.m. sharp Ernst happily embraced me.

"What are you doing here?" he asked.

"I did not get your promised letter. I came to look for you."

"How did you know I would be here?"

"I didn't. I took a chance. But why are you back in Aachen?"

This is what Ernst told me: "My cousin told us to go to the police station in Holland. We needed permission to stay there. Instead they put us right into prison over night. The next morning they drove us to the border and said, 'You have to go back to Germany' and watched while we half walked and half crawled through a cornfield to get unnoticed right back where we had come from. We kept close to the road. When I saw a car coming, I stopped it. It was a taxi. We jumped in fast. At the German border the driver said, 'Go down on the floor!' and said 'Heil Hitler' to the border guard. We were safely back in Germany. Tomorrow we have to buy new passports and try our luck in Belgium. I just hope I get one where the man wears glasses. I had to take my glasses off when we crossed the border into Holland."

They spent the night in my aunt's house. Early the next morning my cousin Heinz drove me to the train to go home to Berlin. Ernst, Kurt and their mother went to the Hotel Adler shopping for passports.

MY GOLD WATCH

We had just informed my parents that we would get married as soon as I could follow Ernst to America. Ernst explained that he would leave first. He would send me the necessary papers so I could emigrate too. Then he turned to my father, "You cannot stay in Berlin either. Do you have any plans to leave?"

My father looked at Ernst, got up and without uttering a word, left the room. This was not a question that concerned him. His philosophy was: "This will pass." He was not the only German Jew who simply refused to believe that Hitler could last. He had survived World War One, was a patriotic German and a law-abiding citizen. He would just wait until it was over.

What did concern him and what made him happy was that I would get married. He liked Ernst. I think secretly he had hoped to arrange a wedding for us. This announcement was as close as my parents would get to our wedding.

To show his approval he bought Ernst a beautiful gold watch. Not being concerned about the political situation in Germany and buying a gold watch for his future son-in-law were characteristic of my father. He was a conservative and generous man. He had not done anything wrong, ergo nothing could happen to him. And he would not do anything wrong now either. My mother and my uncle, his brother, begged him to inform his customers in Scandinavia and Switzerland not to send the money they owed for merchandise to Germany. It was against the law. But it was one way to accumulate money abroad, since it was also against the law to take marks out of the country. Other businessmen did it but he refused to even talk about it.

He was ready to hand over all my mother's jewelry to the government when that suddenly became mandatory. My mother protested. She and I arranged to smuggle it out of the country. We gave part of it to a friend of my future brother-in-law. She was a semi-professional smuggler. She had a Swiss passport. She boarded a train to Brussels and knew that the toilets on the train were locked when it came to the border. She went to the bathroom just before the train stopped for customs and hid the jewelry in the washroom. As soon as the customs officers left and the train was moving again the doors were unlocked, she retrieved the precious stuff. In Brussels she delivered it to my cousin.

I took the train from Berlin to Aachen, a seven-hour ride, to deliver a big diamond pin and a ring to my aunt. She was on her way to Brussels too to visit her daughter. She had a big bosom and wore a colorful flowered dress. The pin was practically invisible on her bust. The ring was hidden under elegant white gloves. The rest I took when I finally exited. I wore a diamond bracelet and had a big gold cigarette case from Ernst in my small carry-on suitcase. None of us was caught. But a few weeks later the Germans got wise to the hiding place in the toilet. The big pin and the cigarette case have remained in a bank safe for the last sixty years! In an emergency they could be turned into cash.

My father's taste was impeccable, though on the conservative side. When my mother and I came home from a shopping trip in preparation for my leaving, I proudly showed him the black lingerie we had bought. He shook his head, "Nice girls don't wear black underwear." However, I always liked the things he bought for me on his various business trips. I still remember the red, white and blue sweater jacket he had bought for me in Vienna. I wore it for many years long before red, white and blue became my national colors. Once my parents brought me three silk blouses from Switzerland. Two I loved. One I never wore. That one my mother had selected. It was embarrassing but peasant blouses were not my style. The other two lasted a long time. I still wore them in New York. I respected my father's taste and he showed that he appreciated my judgment too. He would invite me to help him select silk for future ties. I would proudly sit with him and the salesman who showed us the samples. He would listen to my opinion.

His generosity was not limited to his immediate family. Whenever there was a Bar Mitzvah in the family it was my father who gave the obligatory gold watch. It had become a tradition. My brother was the youngest of seven boys in the extended family. I suppose it was a gentleman's agreement that a father could not give his son the traditional gift. My Uncle Hugo gave Bert the gold watch. He wore it proudly.

A year later my mother's jewelry was estimated for insurance purposes. My father included Bert's watch. I probably would not remember this traditional gift giving and the role my father played in it if Bert's watch had been real gold. But it was "double," a metal that looked like gold. When my father told us about it, he just shook his head. My mother said, "How could he?" and shook her head too, at Hugo's duplicity. I could not understand it. I did not say anything, just thought "poor Vati." The incident was never mentioned again.

Ernst's watch was the last one my father bought. It has become my favored timepiece now. Vati would like that.

FINAL EXIT 1938

I was sitting in the Bolivian Consulate in Berlin. I was waiting for a letter stating that Bolivia would permit me to immigrate to their country. I needed the letter to apply for my passport.

To get a passport I had to prove that another country would accept me. The Bolivians would write such a letter — no questions asked. It was July 1938, and I was twenty-four years old. Ernst, my boyfriend, safely in Belgium, had informed me that in order to be included in his affidavit I had to appear at the American Consulate in Antwerp no later than August the ninth.

At home thirteen big wooden cases with household goods were ready to be shipped into storage in New York. They contained furniture, linen, dishes, and more — enough to furnish a three room apartment. In 1938 Jews were still permitted to take used household goods out of the country.

Two suitcases were waiting to be filled with clothing for all seasons. They would travel with me to Antwerp. Thursday, August the fourth, my passport arrived with the morning mail. Now I could get my visa for Belgium. First I went to buy a train ticket to Antwerp and then I went to the Belgian Consulate.

"Sorry, no more visas for Germans," the man on the reception desk told me.

"I just want to wait for my American visa in Belgium."

"Sorry, no more visas for Germans. New regulations since yesterday."

I rushed home to call Ernst. He had no telephone. I had to call the post office in Knocke, Belgium. They would rush a messenger to his house and Ernst would run to the post office to take the call.

"I'll mail you a special delivery letter tonight."

Friday the fifth I received his letter in the afternoon. "Change your route. Leave Berlin Saturday night the sixth for Basel." (He included all departure and arrival times.) No visa was necessary for Switzerland. I called George and Grete (friends of his I did not know). "George will meet you at the station in Basel and take you to Bern. Monday morning the eighth you go to the Belgian consulate in Bern (in Switzerland they still give visas) and leave Monday night for Antwerp, and arrive Tuesday morning the ninth in Antwerp. Carry a white hanky in your hand so George will recognize you.

I read the letter twice and still did not understand why I could get a visa in Bern if I could not get it in Berlin. If it did not work, I would be stuck in Switzerland with no money and no friends. But I had to take that chance. I informed my parents. They just shrugged their shoulders.

Saturday I tried the Belgian consulate one more time. I asked to talk to the consul.

"I have to be in Antwerp on the ninth."

"Why?"

"To get married."

"Can you prove that?"

"How can I prove it if my fiancé is there and I am here?"

"Sorry, you have to bring proof; without it we cannot give you a visa."

"I will be in Antwerp on the ninth!" I murmured. I did not slam the door, but I was close to it.

I took a cab to the station to change my ticket to Basel. Then I went to the nearest bank to change ten marks into Swiss francs. Ten marks was all I was allowed to take out of Germany. I rushed home to do the last minute packing.

"Did you get the visa?" my mother asked.

"No, but I changed my ticket and got Swiss francs. The train to Basel leaves at 8:30 p.m. tonight."

We sat down for supper. Nobody ate.

At 7:30 we put the two suitcases, my typewriter and a small overnight bag into the car. The two big bags had to be checked through to Antwerp. We did not talk. There was nothing to talk about. I was leaving and they, my mother, father and brother were staying behind. The big question in all our minds was, "When will we see each other again?" Or, worse, "Will we ever meet again?"

Seven people were waiting for us on the platform. My Uncle Ernst and Aunt Lene and their three children, Ilse, Jochen and Walter. My Aunt Evi and her daughter Ursel. Ten people surrounded me, including my brother Bert and my parents. Of all these people, only two survived. My cousins Ilse and Ursel.

My mother held on to my hand.

"Don't forget to send a telegram from Bern, so we know all is well."

"Don't forget to write."

"Sleep on the train!"

"We will meet again on Broadway."

The "all aboard," woke us up. I kissed everyone and went into my compartment. I opened the window. They all looked at me with faint smiles, hankies ready to wave.

"Have a good trip!"

"Sleep on the train!"

"Write!"

"Don't forget to wire tomorrow!"

Slowly the train started to move, very slowly. *I am off. I am leaving. This is for good. I'll never see them again.*

"Auf Wiedersehn. Auf Wiedersehn."

I leaned out the window and waved to them. All I could see were small white sails, getting smaller and smaller. My face was wet, my nose was running. I didn't care. They could not see it. Will they all go to my uncle's house to distract my parents? Will Ernst's friend George recognize me? What if I don't get the visa? My fortune was eight Swiss francs. There won't be any parents to ask for money. There won't be any parents, period! And what about the border tonight? On my left arm I wore my mother's diamond bracelet. I kept Ernst's gold cigarette case in my overnight bag.

The German border control looked at my passport and silently handed it back to me. He pointed to my little suitcase. "Is that all the luggage you have?"

"I also have a typewriter up there." Then he asked the same question again and the woman who was with me in the compartment pointed to her luggage. Without a word he left.

The woman suddenly looked at me and said, "That is a nice bracelet you are wearing." I just smiled at her. I did not want to talk to her. I did not know who she was.

Then I tried to sleep, without success. It was a long night.

We arrived in Basel on time. Clutching my white hanky, I got off the train. It was Sunday, August the seventh.

George saw me immediately.

"How are we getting to Bern?"

"We will be there in an hour. I have my motorcycle here."

"Motorcycle?" I said. "What about my typewriter and suitcase?"

"Don't worry. We'll put them between us."

I spent the night in their house. The next morning, Monday the eighth, Grete took me to the Belgian consulate. At 9 a.m. sharp I rang the bell. A maid in black dress, white apron, and white headband opened the door.

"I would like to get a visa for Belgium," handing her my passport.

"How long do you want to stay in Belgium?"

"Ten days."

"What for?"

"A vacation."

"Have a seat."

Grete sat down. I started to walk the floor. Back and forth and forth and back. A big old-fashioned clock ticked the time away. Very slowly it went tick tock, tick tock. Every tick and tock seemed to be ten minutes long. I walked and walked. Six steps toward the window and six steps toward the door and back again. Finally the door opened. The maid again. She handed me my passport. "That will be 2.75 francs."

I paid her and said, "Thank you." Only on the street did I dare open the little brown book. There was the priceless stamp, "Visa de Tourism." I had enough money left to send one wire to Berlin and one to Ernst.

On Tuesday, August the ninth, at 8:00 a.m. I arrived in Antwerp. Ernst, armed with red roses, was waiting for me on the platform. We picked up my two big suitcases. He took me to the station restaurant for breakfast.

At 10:00 a.m. we were sitting in the waiting room of the American Consulate.

HOW I GOT MARRIED 1938

"**B**rother, you can still change your mind," Kurt said laughingly, while he stopped the car. We were twenty meters from the entrance to City Hall in Brussels on our way to get married. Ernst, my husband to be, was in a solemn mood and with a tinge of anger in his voice, said "Let's go!"

It was September 24th, 1938 and we had to get married. The American Consulate had told us, on August 9th, "Without a marriage license you cannot sign the papers for your visa."

To get married in Brussels we had to prove first that we were single. This proof had to come from Berlin, our last domicile. Our names had to be posted in Berlin's Town Hall for two weeks. Anybody who wanted to object to our plans could do so during that time. My parents in Berlin took care of that. While we were "hanging out" in Berlin we went to a lawyer in Brussels to get a premarital contract. Without it, according to Belgian law, everything I owned would become Ernst's property as soon as I became his wife.

How we found the lawyer I don't remember. What I do remember is that we did not know that we had to come with two witnesses. That did not present a problem. Suddenly the lawyer got up, excused himself and returned with two men he had picked up on the street. They became our witnesses and gladly signed the papers for a slight fee.

Our wedding day had finally arrived and there was nothing romantic about it. The marriage license was just one more step to getting the precious visa to the United States. I did not wear a white outfit. I wore a navy blue silk dress with a matching cape. The dress had white trimming around the neck, the matching navy blue hat had a white ribbon around the crown. My mother had decided that this was the proper outfit for this important day when I got it in Berlin.

"You cannot get married without a hat."

"I never wear a hat," I protested.

"You have to wear this one!" And so I did.

The wedding party consisted of Kurt, my mother-in-law and my cousin Ilse. Ilse was the representative of my family. She was the only one of my relatives in Berlin who had a valid passport that did not have the letter "J" for Jew in it. Besides she looked like a typical German girl. Without the "J" she would have no difficulty getting back into Germany.

Entering City Hall we were led into a huge room where the chairs were arranged in theatre style. Half of them were occupied. We moved into the next empty row. Facing us was a long table at which the Mayor of Brussels sat. On each side of the table stood a soldier in dress uniform with his gun at ease. The couple about to get married stood in front of the table framed by their two witnesses. When they were pronounced man and wife the two soldiers shouldered their rifles and clicked their heels, the noise they made was so unexpectedly loud that it shocked us. Kurt, never short of a wise crack, said "if they start shooting, duck under the chairs." It broke the ice and we all laughed.

When it was our turn we jumped up and pulled along Ilse and Kurt, our witnesses. In a low and solemn voice the Mayor was talking to us in French. I was holding on to Ernst's hand. On cue we both said, "Oui, Monsieur."

Someone handed us the papers and we were married. The ceremony had lasted less than five minutes. I did not feel ecstatic. I was glad it was over. Monday we could go to the American Consulate in Antwerp, sign the papers and get our visas. First, however, we went to my mother-in-law's house for the wedding lunch. It was during this meager meal that the absence of my parents hit me. How would this special occasion have looked if they had only been here?

Ernst cheered me up as much as he could. He frequently referred to "my wife," which sounded funny to me and made me laugh. But I could not wait to get out of there. I was not in a festive mood. When we finally went back to our little one room apartment a sea of red roses was waiting for me. And when I started reading the attached card from my parents the floodgates opened. Not only were they not at my wedding, but I probably would never see them again. All they could do for me was send flowers. They could not protect me anymore, no matter what — I could not run home. Ernst was my protector now. I knew I could depend on him but it did not take the sorrow away.

We went to Antwerp the following Monday, had our physical and signed all the necessary papers.

"You can expect your visas in about three to four months. We will let you know when to return here with your passports."

We were booked to leave from Rotterdam on the Holland American Line the beginning of January. We had made the reservations and paid for the tickets in Berlin before we left; since we did not know when we would get the visas, we decided to exchange the tickets. Our new departure date was February 25th, 1939.

We left Brussels on February 23rd and stayed two days with friends in Amsterdam. When we boarded the Veendam on February 25th, it was my twenty-fifth birthday.

BERT 1939

"Madame, votre frere est la," our landlady in Brussels called out to us. We came back from one of our fruitless walks through the city, looking for my brother. Dutch friends had arranged for Bert's illegal departure. He had crossed the border into Belgium as a helper on a coal truck.

The "professor" on a coal truck? He was called the professor after he got his first glasses at age two — still sitting in his stroller. They were the smallest glasses the busiest optician in Berlin ever made. They sat tightly on his little nose via silk ribbons behind his ears.

My brother was born cross-eyed. Both eyes were hugging his nose. We never knew what he was looking at. The ophthalmologist said that he could not operate until he was six years old. The glasses were for his astigmatism.

On one of his regular visits to the eye doctor I got my eyes checked too. They were not perfect either. Dr. Fehr, however, decided because I was a girl I did not have to wear glasses for the time being. I liked him for that. But it was the 20 mark bill my mother gave him, which I remember most from this visit. For me, age eight, 20 marks was a lot of money. He took the bill and nonchalantly put it into the outside pocket of his jacket. Walking out of his office through the waiting room, which was filled to capacity, I wondered how many 20 mark bills could fit into that pocket.

Bert was called the professor for a long time. Fortunately, he lived up to his title. He was excellent in school and read everything he could get his hands on. I once saw him reading the encyclopedia. He was nine years old.

"What are you looking up?" I asked him.

"Nothing, I'm just reading."

Instead of regular high school, he attended the American School in Berlin. It was a wise move on my parent's part. It was the best way to become proficient in English. Unfortunately he never had a chance to use the language.

When he was twelve years old his title changed. He became "the transportation expert." He knew the routes and stations of every subway, El, bus and streetcar in Berlin. When a new line opened he had to ride it the first day. Friends and relatives would call him for directions within the city and its environs. True to his title he had found our domicile in Brussels.

We started running when our landlady called and waved at us. Bert had finally made it! It was the first of January 1939. My little brother, who actually towered over me, had finally escaped from Germany. It was a perfect way to start the New Year.

He still wore glasses, but he was no longer cross-eyed. When he started constantly bending his head to one side at age four, our family physician felt that his eyes had to be operated on immediately. Otherwise, he warned my parents, he would grow up with his head permanently leaning to one side. Dr. Fehr protested — he was too young! The two doctors consulted. Bert had his first operation at age four and a half, and a second one nine months later, both successful.

On one of my vacations home from boarding school, my mother approached me with a surprising request. "I wish you would talk to Bert about sex," she said. He was twelve and a half and I was seventeen years old.

"Why doesn't Dad talk to him?"

He doesn't want to do it."

"What about you, Mom?"

"I can't do it, you know I can't."

"What about Uncle Ernst?" He was my father's brother. He was always consulted when there was anything serious to discuss with the children in the family. He had been decisive in my going to boarding school. He had called me on the carpet more than once when my grades were not up to par. Apparently he was not up to it either. But I was. I recently had read a book, whose title I don't remember, which informed young people about sex. We all had read it in Juist.

I still see myself sitting on Bert's bed that evening. My heart was beating a little faster and my hands were wet. I started with the easy stuff. How women become pregnant, how sexual diseases are transmitted, and I touched on homosexuality. He listened attentively. As I became more comfortable, I talked about nocturnal emissions and masturbation. He did not ask any questions, just nodded once in a while — and then he thanked me. We embraced and kissed each other before I left the room. That night we became close friends.

Our close relationship made our new living arrangement in Brussels easy. We became kind of a ménage a trois. Bert moved into our miniature apartment, consisting of one room with a bed, a table and two chairs. Next to this room was a space the size of an old-fashioned maid's room. Its furnishing consisted of a big armoire for our clothing, a two flame gas heater and a pear shaped sink with cold running water. It served as dishwasher, bathtub and washing machine. Into this space our landlady had put a cot. The toilet was separated by a door from this space.

We were a happy family for nearly two months. It was the longest time Bert and I ever lived together. Most of our childhood, I had been in boarding school away from home. The two men took a liking to each other immediately. Saturday mornings they would both get up early to go to the Dutch market. They came home with Matjes herring and delicious white bread and we had a feast. In the evening I cooked dinner on the two gas flames in Bert's room. It did not always turn out perfectly, but we ate it and nobody complained.

We went to the American Consulate in Antwerp and tried to get Bert on our affidavit — without success. In spite of that we kept on planning our future in New York together. Suddenly it was in the middle of February. Ernst and I had to leave to catch our boat to Rotterdam. Bert had to stay behind. We helped him move to a cousin's house.

He went with us to the station where we hugged each other for a long time. I boarded the train. Bert stood alone on the platform and waved to us. He was eighteen years old.

ARRIVAL IN NEW YORK
MARCH, 1939

"The Statue of Liberty!" someone yelled The dining room emptied. Everybody raced up the stairs to get the best view of this symbol of freedom. The boat seemed to be tilting. Binoculars appeared and hankies came out. A chorus of nose blowing started. My face was wet too. This long trip across the ocean was framed in tears. Tears of happiness and tears of sorrow.

Twelve days earlier, when we boarded the Veendam, our little cabin was flooded with dozens and dozens of roses. A letter from my parents was attached to them. Another one from my brother was lying on the bed. Ernst had to read them to me. My eyes were flooded. His voice was shaky too. The departure day was my birthday and the letters were not only full of good wishes but also hopeful that we could celebrate the next birthday together again. My tears were now a mixture of emotions: glad to have escaped from Germany and fear of the unknown.

I did not know what I felt. And then I saw New York rising out of the sea. The sun was mirrored in a thousand windows. The buildings grew taller and taller and I grew smaller and smaller. New York looked like a colossal fortress silhouetted against the blue sky. Was this real? It looked like a beautiful stage setting. We had arrived. We had to get off the boat. Secretly I had hoped we would never have to get off.

And I did not want to get off now. I did not mind that I did not have any breakfast. I was not hungry — I felt queasy, scared. I wanted to stay on the boat. A million frightening thoughts filled my head.

What will New York be like?

What will we do when we get off?

Were all the gangster stories true?

And what about the language? Will my school English be enough? All I remembered were the irregular verbs, which Aeschlimiss, our English teacher, had made us recite over and over. What about work? We have to make money.

My cousin Walter had promised to pick us up. That thought kept me going. He was part of home — Berlin. "Little Walter," we called him. He was about five feet tall. He had arrived in New York only six weeks earlier, but to us, he was a native.

For twelve days we had lived without a care on this floating hotel in the middle of nowhere. The food was delicious for those who could make it to the dining room. The lively ocean inhibited appetites. Ernst and I made it every day. My brother-in-law Kurt never got to eat his dinner. Every night he came all dressed up to our table, gave the waiter his order for every course and then rushed out, up the stairs to reach the railing in time. His main intake was the terrible Maggi bullion served every morning as we all lay in deck chairs, huddled in grey blankets, lined up like soldiers. I suspected that some passengers spent the night there, afraid to go into their cabins when the sea was rough. I had taken the advice of our waiter.

"Eat Bismarck herring every meal. It will prevent sea sickness." It worked for me. Ernst drank his beer daily. A man from Munich had recommended it. It worked for him.

As the days passed, the ocean had become rougher, fewer and fewer people came down for dinner. However, two grey-haired American ladies showed up every meal. They were a picture in pastel. They wore a different colored evening dress every night. What fascinated me were the matching shoes and handbags. Pink dress, pink shoes, pink handbag, lilac dress, lilac shoes, lilac handbag and so it went every night. I had never seen pink shoes or pink handbags. I had one evening dress, yellow, no matching shoes or handbag.

Every night we went dancing no matter how rough the sea was. We did not care if the boat was rocking. As long as the orchestra could play we slid around the dance floor, hoping that the sea would be quiet for just one dance. It actually was fun to fight the moving floor.

Standing at the railing now, I remembered the first night on board. I had sat crying in the lounge after dinner. I felt the movement of the boat and suddenly the leave taking became real. I was not going on a vacation. I can't go back anymore — I will never see my family again — I am leaving forever.

And now the forever had started. The Veendam was not moving anymore. Ernst pulled me away from the railing.

"We have to go through immigration," he said. My heart started beating faster. I remembered all my border crossings. They were always a traumatic experience even if all went well. This one was uneventful. I felt better when I saw my cousin.

Walter had rented a furnished room for us on 110th street and Broadway. He was determined to show us New York immediately. After we left our luggage in the room he took us for lunch to a cafeteria.

"I want to initiate you to the American way of eating," he said and proceeded to put some luke-warm food on my plate. I was dreaming of the delicious food we had on the boat and was ready to go to our room. But Walter had other plans.

'Now that you know how the cafeteria works I will show you how to take the subway." Like sheep we followed him and landed at 5th Avenue and 34th Street .

"Look up," he said. "See that building? That's the famous Empire State Building."

I had learned about the Empire State Building in school. I did not care about this or any other building. I wanted to get back to my cabin. Luckily Walter suddenly decided that it was time for us to go back home.

"You are not going back with us?"

"No, I have to stay downtown. Here are two nickels. Go down these stairs, put the nickels into the turnstile, look for the sign "uptown," take that train and get off at 110th Street."

It was not quite that easy. Several times we asked in pigeon English, "Goes to 110th Street?"

The next morning after several unsuccessful tries I got into the bathroom. I had not realized that we had to share it with three other parties. I was hardly back in the room when the landlady knocked on our door. She proceeded to give me a lecture on the purpose and use of shower curtains. I had never heard of shower curtains. But I now knew why the bathroom floor was flooded when I stepped out of the tub. I promised to remember them the next morning.

"We'd better look for an apartment," I said.

"Let's start today," Ernst said, smiling. "And let's buy shower curtains."

MOVING IN 1939

61 Vermiliea Avenue was our first address in New York. For weeks we had walked the streets from 110th Street and up, looking for an apartment. In 1939 there were "vacancy" signs on practically every building. Looking at the different places we learned from experience: look for cross-ventilation, don't rent on the top floor — too hot in the summer, check if the water runs in the kitchen when the shower is used in the bathroom. We finally decided on a three-room apartment in a fourth floor walk up near 200th Street. It was cheap, forty dollars a month, plus the first month free as a concession.

The day we moved in, April 1st, 1939, thirteen huge wooden cases came out of storage and were delivered to our new address. They contained everything and more to furnish a three-room apartment. The grand piano came up first. It took up most of the living room.

"What are we going to do?"

"Maybe we need a bigger apartment?"

"You are crazy."

"Then we have to sell the piano."

"The Bechstein?"

I saw it standing in the corner of our living room in Berlin with its beautiful Persian patterned cover. Nobody played on it. I had stopped taking piano lessons at age thirteen — but it was a vital part of our home and I was attached to it. The piano and a few other precious pieces were my dowry. In an emergency they could be converted into cash. Strictly speaking lack of space was not an emergency but we had no choice. The Bechstein went for one hundred dollars. I was upset when it was picked up. I did not realize that I had an emotional attachment to it. Next came the couches. One with two matching armchairs from our living room. The other one was my sleeping couch, you lifted the top and put the bedding into the bottom.

I could still see Elsa, a young woman who worked in our Berlin household, and my cousin Walter, opening the couch about 1 a.m. one night. Walter had taken me for dinner with an out of town friend of his. We went to Mikosh, a Hungarian restaurant on the Kurfuerstendam. A pianist and violinist played "Schmaltz music." We had wine. Walter's friend bought me a big bunch of roses. I was flattered and animated. Glasses were raised and another bottle of wine appeared. I began to get dizzy, stood up and went outside hoping the fresh air would help. Walter followed me and realized it was time to go home.

When we came to my house, I gave Walter my house key. It broke in the lock. We knocked on Elsa's window and she came to the rescue. They walked me up the stairs to my room. While I was worried about my roses they worried that my parents might wake up. They opened the couch together and Elsa got me into bed and put the roses into a vase. I never forgot Walter's chivalry that night.

Bookshelves and books arrived next. The German classics: Goethe, Schiller, Heine, Thomas and Heinrich Mann, Rilke, Hesse and the collected writings of Shakespeare in German. Dostoevsky, my favorite writer. Some of these books came in handy later when I went back to school. Oil paintings appeared and rugs. Thirteen of them neatly rolled up in heavy paper. We put four down. The rest I kept rolled up in a closet. Years later when I took the paper off they had disintegrated into dust. The moths must have had a real feast.

I brought enough linen to last a lifetime. Sheets, towels, kitchen towels, tablecloths with matching napkins, hand embroidered. Some large enough to set a table for twenty-four. Silver, dishes and glasses to go with it. It was on holidays like Passover that we had fifteen to twenty people for the Seder. In Germany the table was set with white tablecloths, the creases only partly covered by the white plates with their narrow gold and black border. The crystal glasses and the silver candlesticks reflected the lights. My uncle sat on one end of the table. He presided over the Seder. Under a gold embroidered red velvet cloth were three matzos next to his plate. We children had small liquor glasses instead of wine glasses. When everybody had to dunk his pinky into the wine we participated eagerly and sucked the leftover drop from our fingers.

Pots and pans appeared in New York. My mother did not forget anything. Ladles, strainers, a can opener, kitchen knives, brooms, dishrags, soap powder and even a washboard came out of one case. I actually used that washboard in pre-washing machine days and hung the laundry to dry on a pull-up contraption in the kitchen. It was attached to the ceiling. You could eat at the kitchen table without opening an umbrella. I gave the embroidered bed linen to a Chinese laundry. After a few washings it came back torn. No-iron sheets were my first big purchase in New York.

And then the huge silver service set appeared, a big coffee pot, teapot, creamer and sugar bowl and a matching silver tray. It had stood nicely arranged on the tray, on the buffet in our dining room in Berlin. Never used, it just stood there sparkling in the light between two large Meissen porcelain scenes. One depicted a boy leading two cows; the other was a matching piece a shepherd girl with two goats. Since we had neither a dining room nor a buffet in our three-room apartment the silver service went next, for a pittance, eighty dollars. I did not feel good about this sale either. What would my parents say if they knew how little money we got for these things? Besides we were to sell them in emergencies only.

The first emergency arrived when my daughter Ellen was born in 1941. We needed money to pay the ninety dollars for the hospital. Dr. Wiesbader charged eighty dollars. That included pre-natal, post-natal care and the delivery. We could pay him in installments. My mother's mink coat was put up for sale. I got eighty dollars for it. I was glad to get rid of it. I would never have worn it and constantly worried that the moths would devour it.

A few glasses and two Delft tile coffee tables did not survive the trip from Europe. All but twelve of the beautiful tiles were broken. I saved them for twenty-five years. When we moved into our present apartment in 1967, I had a table made from them.

The second emergency presented itself two yeas later, when Ernst was in the hospital. I did not have the forty-two dollars for my rent. The only income I had was from addressing envelopes at home, which barely was enough to feed us. What I did have was a pair of diamond earrings, which my mother never wore. They were too gaudy for her. All she ever wore was one little pearl in each ear. I had no sentimental attachment to the diamond earrings — but I did not want to sell them. I knew I would never get the real value — that much I had learned. All I wanted was the money for the rent.

Bertchen, an older friend and ersatz-mother here, suggested I pawn them. Pawn them, I thought, isn't that something for poor people? And then I realized that that was exactly what I was, a poor person. I had a hard time seeing myself so poor that I had to pawn something to pay the rent. What would my parents say if they found out? Bertchen consoled and convinced me, she even offered to go with me to a pawnshop on 8th Avenue. I was nervous and afraid. I did not trust the entire process but we went.

The atmosphere in the store didn't make me feel any better. One man was arguing with someone behind a gated window. His voice became louder and louder. He walked out of the store visibly angry. On a counter stood a dreary looking couple pricing diamond rings. They were not confidence inspiring either. I was scared and ready to walk out of the store. I looked at Bertchen turning towards the door. She shook her head and pushed me towards the now free window. I could not see the man behind the gate but I handed him my jewels. He looked at them through a magnifier. "How much do you want?"

"Forty-two dollars."

"Okay," he said and handed me the money and a receipt.

"If you don't pick them up within two years we'll sell them."

Those earrings were not in the big wooden cases with the rest of the household goods. Eighteen months later with Bertchen at my side, I went back to the pawnshop. I was as tense as the first time, worrying whether he still had the earrings, apprehensive about going into the dreaded store again. I paid forty-two dollars plus interest and had my jewels back. Many years later the earrings were transformed into what became my favorite ring. Its life saving history has made it an heirloom now.

When Ellen was eight years old we bought a piano, not a grand piano but a little one that fit into the hall of our three and a half room apartment.

I never missed the big silver set. It was too ostentatious for me. But I still see it standing on the Berlin buffet with its vertical wavy pattern reflecting the light.

BERTCHEN

I dialed Bertchen's number every day at 5 p.m. Today was no different.

"Stein residence," the housekeeper answered the phone.

"May I speak to Ms. Kaufman."

"Is that Mrs. Larson?"

"Yes."

"Oh, Mrs. Larson, something terrible happened! Ms. Kaufman just died. The police are here."

"What?"

"Ms. Kaufman is dead. You are the first one to know. I haven't even called the Steins yet."

"Call them!" I said and hung up the phone.

Bertchen dead? I just sat there. Bertchen dead? Gone?! She was my best friend, my substitute mother, my confidante — the one person I could trust implicitly. Whatever happened good or bad I would dial her number to share my happiness or misery with her.

Bertchen Kaufman had come from Berlin a few months after us. Twenty years older than myself, she had never married. In Berlin I hardly knew her, she was friendly with my parents. My mother had told her to contact us in New York.

She quickly found a sleep-in job as a baby nurse and visited us for the first time one Sunday, her day off. She would come back many Sundays after that. Once she arrived with knitting in a big shopping bag. She was knitting a dress to make some extra money. A woman gave her home work and the money came in handy. From then on the clicking of the needles accompanied our talking every Sunday. Once she came with two shopping bags. The second one was stuffed with three dresses.

"Try them on," she said. "Mrs. B. gave them to me. They are your size, they don't fit me."

I was eager to try them on. The first one was bright red with a little white print. The second one was navy also with a little white print. They both fit perfectly with their wide swinging skirts. I liked the red best but wore them both. The third was black, a version of "the little black dress" for all occasions. It was cut straight and seemed tailored just for me. I had that little black dress with its Saks Fifth Avenue label for years. I wore it at parties, weddings and New Year's Eve. I put my mother's diamond pin on it and felt very elegant. It was the only "little black dress" I ever owned.

Bertchen would stay with a family for about three years and then move on to another newborn baby. She never had trouble finding a job. Once I drove her to an interview with a new family, the Steins. I waited for her in the car. She came back full of enthusiasm and started working for them the following week. The baby, Paul, was one month old, and both parents were working. When little Paul was three years old his sister Nora was born and Bertchen stayed on. She remained with the Steins even after Paul got married. A member of the family, she died in their home, which had become her home too.

Bertchen waited for us in our apartment in Inwood when I came home with my baby from the hospital. I carried Ellen in a pink bag, which was closed with a zipper except for a little open space for her head. I was afraid to take her out of the bag. Bertchen took over and put her into a little basket she had borrowed from the people she worked for at the time. She made lunch for us, watched me changing diapers, showed me how to burp the baby properly and gave me other valuable tips on baby care. Between her job and her homework she had found time to knit a little white sweater for my baby. When Ellen was one year old it was Bertchen who bought her first ice cream.

When I had a fight with my husband she would listen to my rage and return me to sanity. When I did not know what to wear or what gift to buy on a special occasion, she came to the rescue. We loved to go shopping together, particularly at Christmas time when the stores were crowded and comment on the kitsch that people bought. Then we would have a comfortable lunch at Lord and Taylor's.

We went to concerts and the opera together. Schmoozing together over a glass of wine after the performance was one of the major attractions of the evening for me. Then I would wait with her for the number 5 bus that took her home to the Stein's in Greenwich Village. I liked it that she lived there. I was attending morning classes nearby at the New School and frequently I would go to her house for lunch, or we would just walk through the narrow streets looking at the store windows or actually going inside. We always found time for a cup of coffee in a quaint place afterwards. It gave us a sense of luxury and a whiff of home — Berlin.

Bertchen proudly attended my graduation at the New School and handed me a bunch of flowers after the ceremony. She was the most generous person I knew. Most of her money went for presents. I still cherish the heart-shaped little enamel box she gave me for one birthday and the silver chain with the perfume bottle pendant. Flowers were her special love. She hardly ever came to my house or anyone else's without a fresh bunch. She was just as generous with the Steins. When she went on her yearly vacation to Germany to visit her friends, she came back with pure linen tablecloth or Rosenthal china for them.

For twenty-five years this slightly lopsided friendship went happily along. Slowly we had become equals, the age difference no longer apparent. When the Stein children were out of the house, Bertchen rented a small studio apartment on the floor below the Steins. She never spent any time there, using it only for sleeping. She took all her meals upstairs, even breakfast. She made herself useful running errands for Mrs. Stein, did some cooking and supervised the housekeeper.

We called each other daily and saw each other frequently. One Sunday night she called at 8:30 p.m. and informed me that she could not come that evening. It was the third Sunday in a row that she cancelled her visit.

"I can't come because the Steins have company."

"You don't have to stay home because they have visitors."

"But I want to be here. I want to know what is going on."

"Nothing is going on," I said annoyed. "You are afraid to miss some gossip, that's all! If Mrs. Stein coughs once you cannot come. It's disgusting!"

"Okay, I won't come anymore!" She hung up.

For a week, I waited for her to call me. She had hung up on me, so she has to call, I reasoned.

I had landed at the bottom of the Totem pole. I was jealous! She was my mother-ersatz first. Mrs. Stein had taken my place. While I didn't need a mother anymore, I still needed her. I needed a dependable friend.

And still I could not make the first call. It seemed to be the end of our relationship. People we both knew kept us informed about each other's lives. For two years we had no contact and then my cousin suddenly died. We met at his funeral. We saw each other immediately, and both smiled. "How are you, Bertchen?"

"I am fine and how are you?"

"I am fine too," and when we took seats next to each other, we did not stop talking until the service began. There was no hesitation. Time had stood still.

I was sad that my cousin had died, but I also felt glad that his funeral had brought Bertchen and me together again. We picked up where we had left off. Called each other daily, made dates for lunch, and went to concerts together. We never talked about the silent two years. Then suddenly Bertchen's health started failing. She had developed a heart condition. The doctor suggested an operation. She refused his advice. We all reasoned with her to have the operation.

"If I become an invalid, I will be a burden for the Steins. I want to die like my mother. She sat in her favorite chair and did not wake up any more."

"Bertchen, please listen…"

"Let's not talk about it anymore. My mind is made up!"

And so it was. We still went to concerts. Afterwards she would wait in a corner protected from the wind, while I ran off to get a taxi for her. To get home by bus had become too strenuous.

Three years after our reunion, one year after celebrating her 75th birthday, she and I went to see "Fiddler On The Roof." As always, I put her into a taxi to go home. It was the last time I saw her.

The next morning she took the dog to the vet. When she returned she asked the housekeeper for a cup of tea. Half an hour later she was dead, her wish fulfilled. She sat in a chair and did not get up again. The teacup lay unbroken on the carpet surrounded by a dark halo.

The Steins gave me her address book and I wrote to her friends in Germany. Nobody answered my letters. But for four years I got a beautifully painted metal box filled with lebkuchen, Pfeffernuessen and stollen for Christmas, a gift she had received every Christmas from her friends in Germany.

I still have the boxes, though I don't need them to remember Bertchen.

FIRST IMPRESSIONS 1941

The first impressions I had of New York were filled with astonishment and sometimes the realization that things were…just different. It was hard to get used to the New World. We would compare it constantly with the old world and many of our sentences started with "*bei uns*," which means at home, or in French "chez nous." *Bei uns* Easter was a two-day holiday and so was Christmas. *Bei uns* the stores opened at 8 a.m. and so did the schools. In the best of times, in Berlin, the Jewish holidays were noticeable because some businesses were closed, but otherwise the non-Jewish community did not take notice of them. If you worked for a Jewish employer you had the day off, and I don't think anybody complained about that. But gentile people for instance did not say "Happy New Year," or "Happy Rosh Hashanah" to a Jewish person.

The first holiday for us in New York was Passover. Fresh flower vendors were on every corner and people would wish us a happy holiday, a pleasant surprise. At other times fresh flowers were a rarity. It was easier to buy artificial ones. *Bei uns* you could buy violets and lilies of the valley on every corner once Spring arrived. And roses and carnations and asters during Summer and Fall. Not many people had fresh flowers in their home here. We were invited for dinner once, and we brought flowers. The hostess had to go to a neighbor to borrow a vase. That seemed a little strange to me, in fact I was embarrassed. Eventually I found out that it is customary to bring a bottle of wine. I always thought if you invite someone for dinner the wine is included! After all it was not a potluck affair. Later when I got wine from friends I often saved it for the next dinner party we were invited to, particularly if I did not like it. The only problem was that I had to be sure that they were not the ones that gave it to me. A bottle like that could go a long way and never be opened.

We ate in the hosts' little dining room. We never entered the living room. Through the open door I discovered that all the furniture in that room was covered with plastic sheets. I never could figure out whether you actually sat on the plastic or whether it came off if people were invited to sit there. Was this a general American custom or a class distinction? I could not picture the Rockefellers with plastic covers on their furniture.

Here is the image we had of the USA: America was the land of sports. However, when we came here nobody actually participated in any sport. The children in school had gym in their street clothing. *Bei uns* children changed into gym outfits and practiced track and field; ball playing was an extra-curricular affair. The newly arrived Jews started their own sport club, a continuation of a club in Berlin. We even started to play field hockey. We took my two-year-old daughter along to the games until she could not be stopped from running after the ball during the game and it became dangerous for her. However, I did win a medal in broad jumping.

Another surprise were the social activities for young teenagers. Dances for these children were held in churches and synagogues strictly divided by religion with the exception of the prom. *Bei uns* events like these would be in schools and if not in schools they certainly were not organized by religious organizations. It was rather strange coming from Nazi Germany to find this kind of division here. In the boarding school I attended, religion was never an issue. I knew some people who were Jewish in the school, but my best friend was not. Nor was my boyfriend. My friends throughout my primary school years in Berlin were definitely mixed if not mostly non-Jewish. My daughter here in New York had only Jewish girlfriends during her school years. In fact, that has just occurred to me - rather strange considering our background.

"Gentlemen's Agreement" was one of the first books I read in English. It was a shock to me. So were quotas for Jews in colleges. It was really hard to fathom. Most of my life I had lived in pre-

Hitler Germany and I had never heard of quotas in schools or restricted hotels. Maybe I was too young to know about it and literally did live on an island. But it was strange and not to me alone. I was equally shocked when I found out about the segregation in the South. Black people lived in Germany at the time too. They frequently were students. No one gave it a second thought. They mingled with the general population. Some had remained from the First World War. Soldiers from West Africa stayed in Germany and married German women. They ended up in concentration camps.

One day a business acquaintance of Ernst invited us to his wedding. I hardly knew him and had a very hard time figuring out what gift to buy. I finally got a pretty vase; thinking of my earlier experience; maybe I could entice them to buy fresh flowers. While we were eating the delicious food I observed the bride going from table to table talking to everyone. Then I noticed that all the men discreetly took a white envelope out of their breast pocket and handed it to her. The bride rewarded them with a shy kiss. At first I did not know what this was all about, until Ernst who was a little faster, told me.

"What?" I said. "They give her a check as a wedding present? And on their wedding night they count how much money they got?" Later it was explained to me that this money is frequently used to pay for the wedding festivities. That made even less sense to me.

"If they can't afford a big wedding why do they have one?" was my argument. "They might as well charge for the dinner." I decided that I would never give money on these occasions. And for about twenty years I kept my vow. Sometimes I was lucky and people were registered, at other times I used my imagination, considered my budget and bought a gift. The first time we gave a check was when our niece got married. I knew she needed money, but I also knew that this money would not be used to pay for the wedding. Slowly I got used to the custom. Today I think of it as the easy way out. You write a check and you don't have to break your head and run around to find an appropriate gift. But I also found out that it is more expensive.

For a long time now I haven't used the term *bei uns*. Instead when I am on an overseas trip, I'll say, "In New York the stores are open seven days a week, in New York you can get decaffeinated coffee in every restaurant, in New York practically every business accepts credit cards, in New York you can pick the fruit you are buying piece by piece," etc.

MY FIRST JOB IN NEW YORK 1939

We had been in New York for three weeks. The apartment was furnished — time for one of us to start work. When Helen, a distant relative, offered me a factory job, I accepted it gladly and considered myself lucky. Many women in my situation could only find work as maids. I had secretly sworn to myself that I would do anything except clean other peoples' bathrooms.

It was easier for women to find jobs. They were nearly always the first ones to work. Physicians for instance who immigrated had to pass difficult tests before they could practice. They also had to take English classes. Their wives usually supported them until they got their licenses.

Helen was much older than I. She had come to New York with administrative experience two years earlier. She was the manager of Alexandra de Markoff, a small exclusive cosmetic factory. The following Monday, I met her on the Dyckman Street subway station at 8 a.m. At 9 a.m. she introduced me to my co-workers. The entire operation, factory, shipping and office, was on one floor in a building on Fifth Avenue, one block north of Rockefeller Center.

My job was to put lipsticks into cases. I had to put the still warm red mass into the metal shells and swish it over a little flame to erase my fingerprints. When I was finished with one color, I glued tiny round labels on the bottom of the cases. Before going home I washed my hands to get the color off — without success. I still had red fingers when I went to bed.

Next to my working space were three French women. They reminded me of witches. They constantly stirred a white mass with a wooden stick in a large pot, brewing the magic face cream. Other women were filling small white jars with it. A third group put tiny burgundy colored silk ribbons around the top of the little containers. The miniature bows were always perfectly tied. It was Alexandra de Markoff's trademark.

Only recently I found out that the company is now a subsidiary of Revlon. The little burgundy bows are still on the jars — but now they are painted on.

I did not improve my English working there; however my French, which we had practiced in Belgium, came in handy. My salary was twelve dollars a week. I budgeted seven dollars for all household expenses. That included sixty cents carfare (I had to work a half day on Saturdays), twenty-five cents for five cups of coffee. Every lunch hour I went to a cafeteria in Rockefeller Center for a cup of coffee and to mingle with "real" Americans. I brought my sandwich from home. Ernst made it for me. It was the same every day. Cervelat wurst, which is a kind of salami, on rye. I ate the identical sandwich for lunch for many years until I went back to school. I never tired of it.

Going out for dinner was not part of our schedule. Our entertainment was listening to the radio. We did not have a telephone but a radio yes; and listening to it was an English lesson in disguise. Walter Winchell was the big challenge. When we could finally understand part of his broadcast we considered it progress. Saturday afternoons I cleaned the house and went marketing for the entire week. I tried to spend a total of one dollar in the fruit and vegetable store. It was the minimum for a free delivery. I rarely succeeded. Three pounds of apples were ten cents and potatoes cost even less. Most of the time Ernst and I carried the bags up to our fourth floor walk-up apartment. It took me twenty years to get my first charge account. My philosophy was; if I don't have the money, I can't buy it. I got my first charge-plate from Lord and Taylor, the department store.

Meanwhile I was still putting lipsticks into little golden cases with my permanently red fingers. After three months on this job, I got rewarded for my diligence with a two-dollar raise. We used this windfall to go to the movies. That was not a luxury. It was the best way to learn English. Ernst was not looking for a job. He was busy finding affordable space to start his own business with his brother before the little money he had smuggled out of Germany in his shoes was gone. They found a loft on East 23rd Street and started manufacturing men's sportswear. They wanted to repeat what they had done very successfully in Berlin.

I reluctantly quit my job at Alexandra de Markoff and became the receptionist, gofer and, with my portable Remington, typist and secretary at "Larson Sportswear." I also got pregnant.

THE BABY IS COMING 1941

My diagnosis "pregnant" was confirmed by Dr. Wiesbader, who became my designated obstetrician. On my first visit to him Ernst came along. Dr. Wiesbader was reassuring, took my history and said, "I want to see you every two months. Today I just need a blood sample."

I watched him pushing the needle into my arm, I never had a blood test before. When the blood started flowing, the room turned around me. I fainted. I had never fainted before or since. It was embarrassing. However I recovered in a few seconds and saw the doctor and Ernst smiling at me.

"Do you feel nauseous in the morning?"

"A little."

"Drink a glass of orange juice before you get out of bed. Your husband has to bring it to you."

Ernst nodded and asked, "What is your fee, Doctor?"

"For pre and post-natal care and delivery it will be eighty dollars. You don't have to pay it all at once. Pay me at your convenience."

"And how much will the hospital be?"

"Beth Israel Hospital charges ninety dollars for your ten day stay."

It was a lot of money for us. However we still had my mother's mink coat hanging untouched in the closet and we did get enough money for it to cover the hospital expenses.

The orange juice in the morning worked. I went with Ernst to the office every day. After two months, the elevator man greeted me one morning with, "Are you going to have a baby?"

"Yes, how do you know?"

"I can see it."

It was time to get a dress in a larger size. I went to Hearns on 14th Street and bought a beige and blue dress in size 14. Two months after that I went back to Hearns and bought a maternity dress. It was navy blue and had colorful ribbons around the neck, sleeves and hem. I did not like it, but it was cheap. At home I wore a multicolored silk suit. I had it made from some leftover tie silk my father had brought home in Berlin. It had very wide pajama-like pants. They fit me for nine months. I borrowed a winter coat from a friend, who was larger than I and who luckily had two coats.

My parents were delighted when they got the good news. They wrote that they were looking forward to becoming grandparents. And then they said, "By the way we have a new address. We moved out of the house and now live in a three room apartment." They did not say why they had moved. It puzzled me.

On my last visit to Dr. Weisbader, he said when I got off the scale, "You are gaining too much weight, we don't want the baby to get too big. I have to put you on a diet, no more cakes or sweets. Eat a lot of fruit instead."

The calculated date of birth was February 15th. In January I stopped working. Since we still did not have a telephone, I called Ernst every noon in the office from a public phone to let him know that I was okay. I packed my little suitcase with a housecoat, nightgowns and toothbrush. I had bought a black jersey robe with a long zipper down the front. I was determined to fit into it after I got rid of my belly. I did.

On February 10th I woke up at 6 a.m. with a bellyache. At 6:30, I woke Ernst. "Please go down and call the doctor. I have pains."

"Are you sure? It's only the 10th today."

"How do I know? I never had a baby before! Call him, he'll know."

He told us to go to the hospital. Beth Israel is on First Avenue and 16th Street. We lived near 200th Street in Inwood. Ernst took my little suitcase and we walked to the Dyckman Street subway station. It was the morning rush hour, but I got a seat. Ernst stood in front of me, the suitcase between his feet. He pretended to read the paper. I felt fine. The pain was gone. Now I worried that the hospital might send me home. I had heard of women being sent home if they arrived minus symptoms. It was not a pleasant thought. I had too much time to think on that long subway ride. I remembered what my mother once told me. "I had a very hard time when you were born. Your father was walking the floor in the living room — praying."

Generally speaking giving birth did not have the best publicity. I forced myself to stop mulling over these stories. Right now it was important for me to get the pain back.

We got off the subway on 14th Street and Eighth Avenue. "Let's take a cab," said Ernst.

"No, I feel fine, the sun is out, let's walk."

We passed Seventh Avenue, quietly. On Sixth Avenue, he said again, "Let's take a cab here."

"No, I am okay."

We walked all the way to the hospital on First Avenue. No pain. Dr. Wiesbader was there. They admitted me.

Ellen, my little daughter was born at 8:20 p.m.

They put me to sleep. I did not feel a thing and woke up in my room. I could not see the baby that night. But Ernst did see her and assured me that all was well. His face was one big smile. He was happy.

"Please send a telegram to Berlin before you go home."

"Tonight?"

"Yes tonight, promise!"

Early the next morning the nurse brought my crying hungry daughter to be fed. While she was happily nursing I counted her fingers and toes and kissed her for the first time. She was okay and now I was very happy too.

Eight months later I received a letter from my parents post-marked in Poland. I did not know then what that meant. But I am grateful to this day that they were still in Berlin that February in 1941.

HOSPITAL 1941

Ernst was lying on the couch in the living room with an unbearable backache. The doctor did not know what to do anymore. He suggested he go into the hospital for Joint Diseases and take aspirin for the pain.

The misery started right after they had to close "Larson Sportswear." Ernst and his brother had worked hard, given it a good try but without success. The little money we had was gone.

Now I had a sick husband, a five-month-old baby and no money. I had managed to get some homework addressing envelopes. The Council of Jewish Women helped us to pay the rent. We still had no telephone. For three days I got the same answer. "We have no bed available, call tomorrow."

I was desperate and afraid to give Ernst the same bad news every morning. He was angry and desperate too. I did not know how to console him. I did not know how to console myself. I had trouble controlling my tears and I was angry, angry at Kurt my brother-in-law and their mother. They knew the situation. They had a telephone. I kept them informed. But they did not visit Ernst and they did not offer to baby-sit. I stopped calling them. I could not afford the nickel every day.

After the hospital said "call tomorrow" for the fourth time, I considered jumping into the Hudson for a second, then I realized that if I could only cry on someone's shoulder, it might help. But the people who could offer their shoulder were not around. Why couldn't my mother be here instead of my husband's? All my problems would be solved. I could work. She would take care of the baby and cook too, but she was not here and never would be. I did not even know where my parents were. The last news I had from them was a postcard via the Red Cross. "We are now in Warsaw," it said but they did not write an address. Luckily I did not know at that time what that meant.

I did know that "ifs" and "buts" did not help. I had to do something. But what? How do you get someone into a hospital if they have no bed? Friends, the Brahms, lived next door. They had convinced me to go to the National Council of Jewish Women for help with the rent. Could the Brahms help me now too? If only with a shoulder to cry on.

"What!" Mr. Brahms said. "They don't have a bed? Then they should go to Hearns and buy one. Do you think if someone has an accident in front of the hospital they won't take him in?"

Mr. Brahms spoke with a Cologne accent. It sounded very funny. I had to laugh.

"I can't fake an accident in front of the hospital."

"Put a coat over his pajamas, take a taxi to the hospital and go into the emergency room. You sit there until they find a bed."

"I can't afford a taxi," came out of my mouth, to my embarrassment.

Asking for money is hard for me. I had trouble even asking my husband. Mr. Brahms handed me two dollars. I accepted them hesitantly. I did not know when I would be able to pay him back. I was embarrassed but also grateful.

Bring the baby over in her carriage with some bottles and diapers," Mrs. Brahms said. "Don't worry about her. She can play with Tommy." Their little boy was three months older than Ellen. I did exactly what they said.

The emergency room was crowded. Ernst sat on a hard chair moaning and constantly trying to find a more comfortable position. I walked the floor, keeping one eye on him and one eye on the nurse at the desk trying to hypnotize her into calling our name — without success. After a three-hour wait, it was finally our turn. They did find a bed. I don't think they bought it at Hearns.

We went into the elevator. *Somebody must have died in the bed a short time ago. I hope they cleaned it thoroughly. If someone died in there it might be a bad omen. I don't want Ernst in a bed where someone died.* These were the thoughts running through my head. The only time I had ever been in a hospital was to have my baby. I was both scared and relieved.

The empty bed was in a ward with seven other men. Four beds lined the walls on each side. Ernst was assigned to the second one on the right. I had never seen anything like this room. Limbs encased in white plaster were hanging from the ceiling. A second later I realized that they were attached to a body. One man had two white legs hanging from a gallows-like contraption over his bed. One had a plastered arm looking down on him. And there was a white plaster head propped up on a pillow. It could have been a crazy sculpture. The head was resting motionlessly. I was scared.

Ernst's spine was stretched in a bloodless procedure. He was in a plaster cast from his shoulder to his hips. He could move his head and arms a little. He did not add to the eerie landscape. He just lay there on his back. Visiting hours were three weekday afternoons and Sundays. Visitors to ward patients had to use a special entrance on the side of the building leading to an outside staircase. We were not welcome in the main entrance. We had to go in through the service entrance.

Every visiting day I appeared with a magic brew. I bought half a pound of lean beef, cut it into small pieces put it into a covered glass jar put the jar into a pot of water and boiled the whole thing for hours. The meat became straw but the brew was concentrated nourishment. Ernst could drink it with a straw. And he liked it.

The hospital was located on 125th Street and Madison Avenue. I had to take the subway from 200th Street and the cross-town bus. The super's wife had volunteered to look after the baby. She had our keys and lived below us. Fortunately Ellen was a good sleeper and asleep when I left.

One evening, in the subway, on my way home from the hospital I suddenly realized that I left my handbag on the bus and with it my entire fortune. Two dollars in cash, a seven dollar check for addressing envelopes, cigarettes and my keys. I jumped up and immediately sat down again — shaking my head in disbelief. What next? What else could possible happen? The super's wife let me into the apartment and lent me fifty cents. The next morning Ellen and I went to the Lost and Found on Third Avenue. They had my handbag. The check, the cash, the keys, the cigarettes and a handkerchief with the initial "R" were all intact. I considered myself lucky — for about twenty minutes.

MORE HOSPITAL 1941

There were no more envelopes to address. I had to get a regular job. The help with the rent from the Council of Jewish Women was all I could accept. I could not ask for more handouts. Through friends I had heard about The Godmother's League, an organization on East 103rd Street that took infants in emergency situations for a limited time. I knew a couple who had left their infant there when the mother suddenly had to be hospitalized. They assured me that the baby would be well taken care of.

I qualified for their services and brought Ellen there. She was seven months old.

After I left her with the nurse, I suddenly saw myself on the train station in Berlin saying "goodbye" to my parents. At least I could visit the baby every Sunday but that did not make this leaving easier. A week is a long time for a baby. I could not contact her or the agency during those seven days. I just hoped that everything would be okay until I could see her again. I had gotten rid of my family. I was free to work. But at what price?

I did find a job with the help of my brother-in-law, Kurt, in a small costume jewelry factory. I had to lacquer ugly pins to give them their final shiny touch at a salary of twelve dollars a week. After work I rushed to the hospital to see Ernst and then went home where I cooked for myself once a week and ate the same thing every night warmed over; soup, meat, potatoes and salad.

On Sundays I went to visit Ellen first. I had to coax her to come into my arms. I had become a stranger to her. I hugged and kissed her but I was not the important person in her life. The nurse had taken my place. When the visiting hour was over, I reluctantly handed her back. Ellen had no trouble leaving me. Smiling, her arms wide open, she went back to the woman while I rushed out the door, fumbling for my handkerchief. Ernst missed the baby too and was eager to hear about her. I assured him that she was fine and well taken care of.

Back home the empty apartment with the empty crib was staring at me. Sometimes I tried to make believe that all this was a dream. But it did not work. It was real! Will we ever be a family again?

Ernst was supposed to come home from the hospital the following Sunday. He practiced walking on crutches. It was not easy with the heavy plaster cast around his torso. The Thursday before that Sunday I got a call at work from The Godmother's League.

"Mrs. Larson, Ellen has a cold. I don't think it is anything serious but we cannot keep her here."

"But I have to work."

"I know, that's why we arranged for her to be admitted to the Hospital for Joint Diseases. It will be easier for you. You have to pick her up tomorrow morning and bring her to the hospital."

"Okay," was all I could muster. I stood there nailed to the floor. How sick is she? If she just has a cold, she does not have to be hospitalized, what could possibly be wrong with her? I fretted.

I decided to call Dr. Dingman, our pediatrician. He knew her from birth and knew our situation and more than once "forgot" to mail us a bill.

"Can I make a call?" I asked my boss who had listened to my conversation and knew our circumstances.

Dr. Dingman consoled me. "They have to be careful, they don't want the other children to catch the cold. I am sure there is nothing seriously wrong with her. Don't worry and keep me informed."

I had to call my brother-in-law, he and his mother were the only relatives I had. "Can I make another call?"

"Go ahead."

I reached Kurt at work and told him the news.

"I'll send Vera (his future wife) to you after work. She can stay overnight and can go with you tomorrow morning. Don't worry."

I wished people would stop telling me whether I should worry or not. I was shaking! I turned around to continue lacquering the damn pins.

"Ruth, you owe me ten cents."

"What?"

"Did you just make two calls?" The boss was a friend of Kurt's.

"Yes, I did."

"Well, you owe me ten cents for the calls." I handed him a dime. What next? Ernst in the hospital, the baby sick and the "friend" wants ten cents for two emergency calls. How I got through the rest of the working day I don't know.

I went to visit Ernst in the hospital but did not tell him the news about Ellen. Then I went home. Finally alone, I could not cry and could not eat. I smoked and walked through the lifeless apartment back and forth talking to myself. "What am I going to do? Well, what am I going to do??? This was not in the script. I was prepared to do any kind of work — but sickness, who ever thought of one of us getting sick?"

I kept on walking and smoking until Vera arrived. In the morning we picked up the baby and brought her to the hospital. The doctor checked her thoroughly.

"I cannot find anything wrong with her. We cannot keep her here."

I was happy that nothing was wrong with her. If I only could take her home and be a mother again. But I couldn't. I also could not control my tears. All I could think was, "what am I going to do?"

Vera took over and asked the doctor to call the Godmother's League. He did and then informed us that they would keep her over the weekend. Ernst and Ellen were now in the same building separated by two floors, though neither of them knew it.

When Ellen was three months old we had moved to Dongan Place and now had an apartment on the first floor close to Ft. Tryon Park. Now I thought if I jumped out the window of our apartment, I might break a leg. For my convenience maybe they would put me in the Hospital for Joint Diseases on a floor between my husband and my daughter. Then we could all be under one roof.

Instead I went to work. It was Friday. On Saturday I visited the baby first and then went down two flights to visit Ernst. On Sunday I visited Ellen first and then went down to take Ernst and his crutches home.

"I'll go with you to visit Ellen this afternoon."

"No, you are too weak. Next Sunday you can see her."

I left the house that Sunday afternoon as if I were going to East 103rd Street, to the Godmother's League. Instead I went to friends nearby for two and a half hours. When I came home I reported about Ellen. Monday morning before going to work, I picked up the baby from the hospital and brought her back to East 103rd Street.

A week later I was fired. My work was not up to par. Through the grapevine I found a job in a small shoulder pad factory. The pay was the same. But the dust was unbearable; even with facemasks we could hardly breathe. But I was not complaining. I got my money on Fridays.

Ernst was able to manage alone at home. The day he went to the hospital to have his cast removed he called me at work. "I have to go back into the hospital tomorrow. The bloodless procedure was not successful."

He had to have another operation. During his stay in the hospital the second time, I rented one of our rooms to the parents of a woman I knew. They worked during the day and ate dinner in their daughter's house. They paid me seven dollars a week. The empty crib went into the living room.

Again I visited Ernst regularly and sometimes even had time to make the magic soup and Sundays I saw the baby for a short hour.

Ernst's convalescence went well. He again came home on crutches and in a cast. After four weeks the cast came off and he could walk with a cane. Best of all I could bring Ellen home since he was able to take care of her during the day. After three long months I finally could pick up the baby. I still see us sitting on the bus. She wore a white running suit, which I had inherited from someone, she was sitting on my lap smiling and flirting with everyone. It was a happy trip. We all slept in the living room. Ernst and I on the couch.

When Ellen started teething and cried during the night, a neighbor complained and suggested I close the window; instead I moved into the crib with her. She stopped crying and all three of us could sleep.

Ernst was hustling to get some bookkeeping work that he could do at home and finally succeeded. He began taking courses in accounting and slowly began not only taking in work as a bookkeeper but also as an accountant. He made enough money so that together with the seven dollars rent subsidy, I could give up my job. I became a mother again. I took Ellen out into the park, fed her, tucked her into bed and kissed her good night…every night.

CONTEMPLATIONS

We had been preoccupied with getting out of Germany. Nobody thought about what would happen once we got to New York. The main thing was to get there. We did not realize that was only half the problem. The other half awaited us in New York, and not just for the first few weeks or even months. We would work at any acceptable job, and everything would be okay. Suddenly nothing was okay.

First there was the language. I had a base of school English and had taken some private lessons before I left Berlin. But I could not read a newspaper, did not understand a word on the radio and even had a hard time talking with people in stores. What was missing mostly, however, was a support system. I only realized that when Ernst got sick.

I envied other women who were able to immigrate with their parents. Their mothers took care of the children and everybody could go to work peacefully. My mother- in-law was here, but I would not and could not trust her with Ellen. She never even offered to baby-sit for a few hours.

I don't remember how many times I thought; "If only my parents were here!"

It was during this time that I got a letter from my uncle dated April 2, 1942, informing me that my parents were put on a transport to Poland and a letter, also via the Red Cross, from my parents dated August, 1942. It said: "We are in Warsaw now. We are fine." That was all it said. No return address.

I did not know what this move to Poland meant. Nobody did. Nobody knew about Concentration Camps either. If I had known, would it have been worse because I could not help them? I shudder and feel guilty and still think maybe we could have gotten them out, maybe we didn't try hard enough, maybe — the "maybes" hound me to this day.

I was upset then, upset that I could not contact them. I rationalized: once the war is over we will hear from them again. I was glad that at least they knew that the baby was born. But they also knew that Ernst was in the hospital and probably worried about that. However, I had not informed them about our desperate financial situation. They could not help us. It did not make sense to burden them needlessly.

I consoled myself with the last words in my parent's letter, "we are fine." With those words they somehow had given me permission to go on with my life. Instead of worrying about them I could continue to worry about Ernst and Ellen. And I did. And I worked. I never did hear from my parents after the war. The letter dated August, 1942; "We are fine" was the last sign of life from them.

Did we know what awaited us in New York? No, of course not. We knew we had to make money. We worried about the language and the gangsters we had heard about. We were optimistic, maybe naïve. But how could we anticipate illness or hospitalization? And how could we know what the move of my parents to Poland meant?

In hindsight, I believe it is better in fact not to know the future. It was easier to take one hurdle at a time, hoping that each new one will be the last one. I don't know what the last one was. Most likely it was not a hurdle at all — Things just slowly improved, very slowly.

MY MOTHER-IN-LAW

When I first met her, Ernst's mother lived in Berlin with her sons in a big luxurious apartment. It was like a bachelor's pad, they each had a room and shared the living and dining areas. Their mother did the cooking and had a woman to clean the house. One evening, I was invited over to dinner to be introduced to her. She looked young and attractive, wearing a black dress with pearls. Her hair was professionally dyed blond, her make-up was apparent but not exaggerated. Right after dinner she left to meet her date. Ernst's parents were divorced when the boys were in their teens and their mother had led an active social life ever since. Until the day she died, there was always a man around. When we all lived in Brussels, she told us she was seeing someone from Berlin. We never met him.

The three Larsons were the first to reach Belgium. After I arrived in Brussels and Ernst and I started preparations to get married, his mother took him aside one day and told him in confidence that I had a dreadful gland disease. Years later, when Kurt was about to tie the knot she told him that his fiancee, Ruth-Vera, had T.B. She even tried to involve me in that deception. Her fantasy had been that each of her sons would marry a rich American girl, preferably a Rockefeller. Unfortunately, we did not meet these standards.

On the boat coming over from Rotterdam, Kurt shared a cabin with her. We saw my brother-in-law a lot, but she did not show up once on deck or in the dining room. Kurt had to bring food for her to their cabin. Miraculously she reappeared alive and well when we landed in New York.

I was always embarrassed when I was with her. She looked like a "Schiessbuden Figur," a mixture of circus performer and bag lady. On the rare occasions she visited us, Ernst would call his brother first, to be sure she looked presentable. Her home-dyed strawberry-blond hair was bordered with white. Her red painted cheeks, her charcoal black eye shadow, and her shining face reinforced this strange appearance. Vaseline had become her magic lotion. She wore it day and night. You could not overlook her even though she was no taller than four feet eleven.

Another bone of contention was her birthday. All her papers said January 19th. When we called on the 19th, to congratulate her she was insulted, "My birthday was two days ago." We argued. But she insisted that all her papers had the wrong date. The following year we called her on the 17th: this time it was two days too early. I once asked her what she wanted for her birthday.

"Just don't bring me any flowers, they are a waste of money."

"Okay but what do you want? Maybe a night gown?"

"I don't need night gowns. I sleep in my old summer dresses. And by the way," she told me when I was pregnant, "don't let anybody bring you flowers when you have your baby."

Her queer dressing habits started in New York. Even later, when she could afford to buy new clothing, she refused to waste money. Once she arrived in an old blue taffeta dress to go to the park with the baby and me. I guess taffeta was not comfortable enough to sleep in! With the taffeta dress, she wore a pair of worn-out black pumps and brownish stockings loosely flopping around her legs. It all went with the shining Vaseline face and the bright red cheeks.

In spite of her appearance, she managed to meet a kind gentleman, Ralph, who soon became her steady companion — where and how she met him we never found out. But he was a nice person who obviously cared for her.

One evening, however, we were all privileged to see her well dressed, actually looking attractive. She had invited us to a party to celebrate her engagement — not to Ralph — but to someone we had never heard about nor would ever see or hear about again.

She did not tell us what happened. Ernst pressed her. "He was a crook," was all she said. Before, during, and after this engagement, Ralph waited patiently in the wings and promptly took her back.

Many years later, she got engaged again. This time without a party. It was supposed to be a surprise for Ernst, Kurt, Ruth-Vera and me. The four of us had gone away for a weekend. My father-in-law had come for a visit from Germany and stayed in Kurt's house. When we returned on Sunday night, the parents, divorced for many years, sat happily smiling on the couch. My mother-in-law jumped up, embraced Kurt and said, "we are engaged."

"So when will you get married?" Kurt managed to say.

"We have not set a date, but soon."

"Soon is a good idea," Ernst said cynically.

We all knew she was unpredictable. But my father-in-law? He was an intelligent and rational man.

"What is her secret?" I asked Ernst, "Maybe I can learn something from her."

A week later my father-in-law announced the annulment of the engagement. And she went back to Ralph.

She spoke to Kurt every day to Ruth-Vera's annoyance. Ernst hardly ever called her. I was the one who had to do the mandatory weekly telephoning. She would answer the phone with a lively, "Hello."

"Hi, mother." When she heard my voice her voice went down an octave.

"Who is this?"

"It's me, Ruth."

"Oh, Ruth-Vera."

"No, the other Ruth. What's wrong?"

"Nothing."

"You don't sound so good."

"I am all right. How is the child?"

"We are all okay."

"Thank you for your call, goodbye." By now her voice was so low I could hardly hear her. On the rare occasions she called us she immediately asked for her son.

"I have something to discuss with you, Ernst," was the usual introductory sentence in her most adult voice. "Why don't you come with Ruth and the child for coffee Sunday afternoon?"

"What's the problem?"

"I have to sign a new lease. I want you to read it first." At other times it might be an insurance problem or taxes.

That she was not even a good grandmother bothered me the most. I was envious of families where a grandmother baby-sat, spoke German with the children, cooked and took care of the house while parents worked. How often did I think, "why can't my mother be here to help out?" It just did not seem fair. On the rare occasions she came to see the "child" she did not even bring a lollipop. When Ellen had a birthday she gave me money. "Buy something practical for me — no toys!" A birthday card was a waste of money. When the economic situation improved for all of us she became more generous. When Ellen graduated from high school, she said: "Buy her a gold bracelet for me."

"You want to go with me?"

"No, just tell me how much you spend and I'll give you the money back."

I did as I was told and missed my mother even more. She would have loved to go shopping for her granddaughter.

We were all grateful that Ralph was around. He did take a load off our shoulders. When they decided to share an apartment, we helped them find one. And when they went to settle in Florida, Kurt helped with the move. We continued with our weekly calls. Kurt went to see them occasionally. It was a relief, no more visits to her house on occasional Sunday afternoons for coffee and cake. I dreaded those, her apartment was dark and stuffy, the coffee bad and I never felt sure if the cups were clean.

Three years after the move to Florida she and Ralph both died in the same hospital a week apart. They were buried next to each other.

She was eighty-seven years old. Ralph was younger. His age remained a secret.

OOMPHIES 1943

I was sitting next to the duplicating machine — crying. It was lunchtime and my second day on the job. For weeks I had tried to get work following "no experience necessary" ads in the *New York Times*. I arrived at 9 a.m. to apply for the job and got the same answer every time "Sorry, the job is filled." I could not understand how the job could be filled at 9 a.m. It was 1943, and I needed work. Ernst did not make enough money to support the family. He had taken courses in accounting and started to work as an accountant at home.

I had everything organized. Ellen, not quite two years old, was picked up by car in the morning to attend my friend Lilly's nursery school. She was not totally toilet trained — but Lilly did not mind. She was glad to have an additional child, and I was glad that she accepted her. At 6 p.m. Lilly brought her to the 181st Street subway station. Ellen walked through the turnstile and we got on the next train to 200th street. I saved a nickel that way.

I finally gave up on the *New York Times* in my desperation. I had told everybody I knew that I needed a job, any job, when a friend told me that Oomphies, a lady's slipper manufacturer, was looking for someone in the office, "no experience necessary."

The next morning I took the subway to Varick Street.

"I am sorry, the job is filled," the receptionist said.

"Are you looking for work?" a man standing behind her asked me.

"Yes."

"Come in." He led me into his office and closed the door. It was Mr. Weinberger, the big boss.

"Where are you originally from?"

"Berlin."

"I am from Berlin too," we smiled at each other and I felt better — like home.

"Would you work in the factory?"

"Yes, anything."

"You'll hear from me," he said and sent me home. He called that evening.

"Come in Monday and ask for Margot in the office."

On Monday, Margot led me to the duplicating machine.

"These are the tickets for the piece workers," she said. "The tickets are numbered. Be careful because each ticket has to be cut up. Each worker gets paid according to the number of little strips he or she has. If you spoil a ticket you have to cancel the number in this book." She proceeded to put a typed master sheet into the contraption, then cranked it by hand and out came a perfect print of the master sheet. It looked easy, but when I tried it, it became very difficult. I was busy canceling numbers in the book. That was easy. From twelve tickets one had come out right. I tried the next bunch — they came out crooked too. Margot went through the procedure with me again. No luck!

Now on my second day I was sitting next to this devilish machine crying. "No experience necessary." What is wrong with me? Why can't I learn to operate this stupid machine? I need this job! I have to learn it! But I was afraid to try it again. I did not want to destroy any more tickets, and I could not face failing again. I just sat there wiping my eyes hoping for a miracle so they would not fire me.

Margot came over. "Be patient," she said. "I am sure you'll get the hang of it. Take a rest and try again after lunch."

I did and somehow in the afternoon the tickets miraculously came out perfect. For three weeks I sat at the duplicating machine turning out perfect work tickets. I got my eighteen dollars every week. That was the important thing. It did not matter to me what

I did. Soon I was advanced to the order department. A new girl, Irene, was put at the duplicating machine. I became her empathetic teacher when she did not catch on right away either.

In 1944 shoes were rationed, and slippers were in great demand. The company grew, and I grew with it. I became the head of the order and shipping department. We had more orders than we could fill. When November came it seemed that every woman in the U.S. wanted house shoes for Christmas. Suddenly I was in a power position. I could decide who got a shipment and who didn't. We got wires from all over the country asking for slippers. I got calls from buyers of big department stores, like Marshall Fields in Chicago. They would cajole and compliment me "You have such a cute accent, I just love to hear you talk." This sweet talk actually worked. I promised them a delivery for the next day. When I was in a quandary, I consulted my boss.

"Who screams the loudest gets them," was his philosophy. "It's the law of the jungle. We can apply it here too." I had my own system. If I promised a shipment that promise would be kept.

One of the consequences of this crazy holiday season was that I got a lot of Christmas gifts from happy customers and happy salesmen. One gave me a beautiful handbag, which I carried for years. Another one surprised me with a sterling silver compact. Plus lots of perfume and candy, even wallets. Ernst asked me every night, "And what is the loot today?"

The day before Christmas, Mr. Weinberger and Mr. Gessner, the two bosses called me into their office and handed me a check for five hundred dollars, my Christmas bonus. At the time, five hundred dollars was a fortune for me. Speechless, I did not know how to thank them, I stuttered something and ran to the telephone to call Ernst.

That same year, Oomphies had its first big Xmas party. Ernst and I arrived late. We had to wait for the babysitter. We were the only sober people in the crowd. Everyone was eager for us to catch up. I finished every glass that was handed to me. After half an hour, I suddenly had trouble keeping my balance and everything was turning around. I was holding on to Ernst to keep from falling. He decided it was time to go home. With the help of a friend they maneuvered me into a taxi. Ernst was annoyed, he was sober, I was worried what the babysitter would think of me.

I had become part of the Oomphie family, and I was happy with my job. I had learned a lot of geography. I knew the big cities in every state and the respective big stores in those cities. I learned how to work our switchboard with its complicated plugs. I was reminded of my final oral exam in school where I had to explain the workings of the telephone.

On Saturday, Oomphies was open, but only half the crew had to come in. When it was my turn I usually sat at the switchboard, and brought along Ellen who kept everyone from working. Last but not least, my English had improved enough to be assigned to work with the buyers that came to our showroom. I loved it. I proudly introduced them to our new line and took the orders. Occasionally they would comment on my accent. "Are you French?" I was once asked. I took that as a compliment and wished it were true. I did not know how to react to it. I did not want to say, "No, I am German." I had no desire to be identified with Germany. But I also did not want to say that I was a German refugee. I just smiled and changed the subject fast.

My main responsibilities were getting incoming orders into production, overseeing the shipping department and taking care of customers' mail. It had become a big job, and I acquired a secretary, Florence. She was young, blond, single, Irish and full of sex appeal. She became the darling of our salesmen. When they were around for meetings, one would always ask her to have a drink with him after work. She happily accepted the invitation and reported on her experience the next day. Invariably the men tried to get her drunk, but she could hold her liquor better than any of them.

"They don't know that I have a wooden leg," was the hysterical punch line every time. We all got a real kick out of it and waited with great anticipation to see who would ask here out the next time.

I seemed to do a satisfactory job judging by the Xmas bonuses I got every year. The fact that I did not have the usual office skills like shorthand and typing was never questioned. My four-finger typing was good enough for the little I had to do.

One summer when his secretary was on vacation, Mr. Gessner asked me if he could dictate a letter to me.

"I don't know shorthand," I said. "But I can write fast."

"Come in." While I was scribbling as fast as I could, he looked over my shoulder.

"Why did you say you don't know shorthand? It looks like shorthand to me."

"It isn't, it's longhand. I better type it right away, otherwise I won't be able to read it myself!" Luckily I remembered most of it by heart.

Everything went smoothly until one November when the Lima Bros. incident occurred. Lima Bros. was a department store in Puerto Rico. Their big order had to be cut separately. In a regular case of 36 pairs of slippers the majority of sizes were 6-7 and 8. For Puerto Rico, at that time, most of the sizes had to be 3-4 and 5. The merchandise was ready to go, all we needed were the shipping instructions from Puerto Rico. (Every customer had to give these instructions.) For two weeks, first thing in the morning I would hear the question: "Any news from Lima Bros.?" And for two weeks my answer was "Not yet." The men in shipping got impatient and so did I. The merchandise was standing around taking up space. Three weeks had passed and again "Any news from Lima Bros.?"

"Ship them Railway Express!" I said and they went out immediately. The second mail brought the long awaited letter. The instructions were not Railway Express. Only then did I realize what I had done. I knew I had to get the shoes back. I called Railway Express. They were on their way to Boston. I called Railway Express in Boston. They had not yet arrived. "When they do arrive please return them immediately to us."

I informed my boss, Mr. Weiser. He didn't say much but called me every half hour "Where are the slippers, Ruth?"

They finally got back to us the next day. Lima Bros. received them in time for their Xmas business. A day later Mr. Weiser called me into his office.

"Ruth what happened? Why did you ship the shoes Railway Express?"

"I really don't know. I don't understand it myself." And I didn't. But it did bother me. I had lost patience and with it my sense of reality. I had acted on an unreasonable impulse and did not even realize it.

KURT MY BROTHER-IN-LAW

It was 1:30 p.m. I just had returned from lunch looking at the work that had piled up on my desk when the phone rang.

"Can you meet me after work?" It was Ruth-Vera, my brother-in-law's girlfriend.

"Sure what's up?"

"You'll find out." Her voice was edgy. She sounded hostile.

"Can you be here by 6 p.m.? I'll wait for you downstairs."

"Okay." It can't be me she is angry with. I just spoke to her two days ago and everything was fine. It's Kurt, it must be Kurt. He and Vera had been intimate friends for four years. She wanted to get married. He did not make a move. He lived with his mother in Queens. She shared an apartment with a friend in Manhattan. Kurt was my mother-in-law's favorite. She did not want him to get married. She would try anything to stop it. Was she up to her old tricks, inventing a disease afflicting Ruth-Vera. Or was Vera pregnant? No, she would never pull a trick like that. She was an up-front person. If you did not know her, she appeared cold but we knew each other and had a warm and trusting relationship. Dirty tricks were Kurt's department. But why was she short with me? I could not concentrate on my work.

Thinking of my brother-in-law and what I knew of him, I remembered our last New Year's Eve in Berlin. Ilse was Kurt's girlfriend then. I had met her many times and liked her. The minute I arrived at the party Ernst whispered, "Rosa is here." Then minutes later Ilse appeared. I did not know Rosa, only that she was Kurt's former girlfriend. She had come from Basel, where she now lived, to spend New Year's Eve with him. He must have been in contact with her. But did he know she was coming? Or was it a surprise, as he now claimed? He got out of this ticklish situation. He planted himself behind the bar for the rest of the night. He cheerfully handed out drinks to every one — mostly to himself. At 12 o'clock he claimed to be drunk and kissed both women passionately. Ernst and I brought Ilse home. Rosa stayed in their apartment. Ilse remained unaware of this precarious situation. In fact, the last time I saw her in Berlin, we had jokingly talked about becoming sisters-in-law.

Could Kurt carry on with two women again? In New York?

I was trying to get my desk cleaned up. My thoughts interfered with my work. I still could not understand why Vera seemed angry with me. I liked her. I was her friend. I did not want her to be angry with me. I could not force Kurt to marry her.

Only two days ago the four of us had driven to the country in Kurt's "new" third-hand car. He could afford to buy an old one, as he could fix anything. He was the handiest man I ever knew. His first job in New York was repairing sewing machines. He had learned that skill in Berlin, repairing his mother's machine. He was so good at it that it developed into a regular business. When later he moved to New Jersey, he not only repaired sewing machines, he also sold new ones. On this outing we had to cross the George Washington Bridge. Twenty yards before we reached the tollbooth, he suddenly opened his door and let his foot drag on the road.

"Kurt, are you crazy?" we screamed.

"The brakes don't work too good. I want to be sure I can stop for the toll." We got a good laugh out of this joke. But was it a joke? I worried about the brakes for the rest of the trip. I never knew whether he was serious or joking. The fact was he put his foot on the brakes whenever a traffic light appeared in the distance — no matter what color it was.

Kurt was a great "smooth talker." Nothing seemed to upset him. He had plausible excuses for not getting married: "I can't leave my mother alone in Queens." Or later: "We first have to find an apartment for her in Manhattan." Vera had fallen for the glib excuses. She did not seem to notice that nobody looked for an apartment.

Thankfully, it was 5:30 p.m. at last. I took the subway up to 40th street. The minute Vera and I met she shouted: "Why didn't you tell me?"

"Tell you what?"

"You knew that Kurt is married!"

"What?"

"Don't pretend you don't know. He got married to Rosa in Brussels."

"He married Rosa? I can't believe it." When could they have gotten married? They lived with his mother in Brussels. I knew there would have to be a lot of paper work involved. I had gone through it. And why didn't they tell us? And how did Kurt manage to leave her behind? And then I realized that she did not have a visa to get into the U.S.A. Kurt knew that, and of course she knew it too. But then why did they get married? It just did not make sense.

"How did you find out?"

"He told me last night."

"He told you last night after four years?"

"Yes. And I don't believe that you did not know."

Why am I accused of doing something unscrupulous? It had happened once before. Anne, my friend for thirty years, wrote to me from Bloomington one day that she never wanted to hear from me again. She claimed that I had an affair with her husband while he was in New York for a week. "Don't write to me! I will not open your letter!"

Six months later I heard from her again. This time she wrote: "I made a mistake, please forgive me." I did.

"What made him tell you last night?"

"I gave him an ultimatum after he came up with one of his smooth excuses again. You know, not being able to leave his mother." What kind of person is Kurt? How could he deceive Vera for four years? How could he face her every day? How could he keep on lying for four years?

Maybe she would be better off not marrying him? For a moment I contemplated that thought. It was not my decision to make. She loved him and she wanted him.

"What is going to happen now?"

"He promised to initiate divorce procedures with the help of his father in Germany. He begged me to wait for the divorce to come through so we can get married."

"Are you going to wait?"

"I waited for four years. It can't take that long to get that divorce, now that the war is over."

"I don't know."

"What would you do?"

I hesitated a moment. "I don't know. Maybe I would and maybe I wouldn't wait."

It took a year and a half for the divorce to come through. Four weeks later they were married.

For three months, I waited for Rosa to appear in New York. I never found out what happened to her, and never heard from Ilse after we were in New York. Vera and I remained close friends until she died of cancer in 1992.

WINNIPEG 1946

I was finally able to visit my Aunt Clara and her family in Canada. They were my closest surviving relatives. Aunt Clara was my mother's only sister. After two days and one night on the train I arrived in Winnipeg, on time, but nobody was at the station to pick me up. With my heavy suitcase in tow, disappointed and upset, I searched for a telephone when I heard someone calling my name. I turned around and saw my cousin Heinz, my cousin Herta with one child in her arms and another one holding her hand trying to keep up, and Herta's husband, Arthur, all running towards me. I started running too. I was so glad to see them. They had been waiting at the wrong station and were as relieved as I was. I had spent many school vacations on their farm in Warden, a little village near Aachen. Now I would visit them on their farm in Canada.

Arthur, their son-in-law, who bought and sold horses in Germany and later in Belgium, had managed to get the entire family into Canada which would grant visas to people willing and able to work the land. There were eight in the family: My aunt and uncle, their three children, Heinz the eldest, Mirjam the youngest, who still went to high school, Herta and her husband Arthur and their two little boys.

We all piled into Arthur's third-hand car for the one hour ride to the farm. I sat in front between Heinz and Arthur. I remembered my uncle's farm in Warden. As children Herta and I would sit together in the outhouse. It was built for two, one hole regular size, one small for children. We always had a wonderful time talking and giggling until my aunt chased us out. They got indoor plumbing in Warden only after my mother threatened my uncle, "I will never come for a visit again if you don't build an inside bathroom."

Arthur, the family joker, suddenly said: "You know, Aunt Clara has been cooking and baking for a week in preparation for your visit. She even killed a home grown turkey, but don't eat it."

"Why not?"

"It was sick."

"What disease did it have?" Arthur was saluting every horse we passed during this conversation and then said: "I told her you don't kill a sick turkey, but she did it anyway." We all laughed and had no idea what he would come up with next.

In Germany he once gave his father-in-law a box with newly hatched chicks. All twenty grew up to be roosters. Nobody could explain how he knew that. In the car, Arthur kept saluting horses and warning me about the sick turkey. After an hour's drive we arrived at the farm. When I stepped out of the car he whispered, "Don't eat the turkey, it was cross-eyed."

After an emotional and tearful greeting we all went into the dining room for dinner. A big roast turkey, meatballs, three kinds of vegetables, potatoes in all different colors. For dessert my aunt had baked an apple pie, a marble cake, and a wonderful cheese-cake, my favorite. It was a meal that reminded me of home. I felt I had a family again.

And then they began to tell me about their experiences on the farm. They had been given the house and some land in the middle of nowhere. I don't know if they paid for it. Arthur said they had to cut the grass first to be able to enter the house. Electricity was only downstairs in the kitchen and dining room. The bathroom was an outhouse. Even today they had only cold running water in the kitchen. The heat in the summer was unbearable and the cold in the winter very expensive.

They had bought a few milk producing cows but could not sell the milk because it did not pass the government test. They gave it away or drank it themselves.

It was particularly hard for my uncle. While he had to be forced to build a bathroom in Germany, his stables there had the most modern equipment, which was missing here. He never really understood why he had to live on this miserable farm, in a strange country where he did not understand the language. The hot summers were particularly hard on him. He would put a cabbage leaf on his head when he went to the outhouse to protect himself from the sun and to keep cool.

My aunt raised turkeys. She told me that the chicks were too dumb to find the food on the ground. Only when she dropped the crumbs over their heads would they open their beaks and with luck one of the crumbs would hit its goal. They were not only stupid but also very sensitive to cold. She kept them in a carton on the kitchen stove. Adult turkeys were sturdy and could survive any weather.

After a year of hard work, the milk finally passed the test. Aunt Clara was in the turkey business and Arthur was busy buying and selling horses. He did well and had moved his little family into their own house, a mile away from his in-laws. His horses were on a separate farm.

Everything was going well in their new house; they even had inside plumbing, until suddenly it caught fire. All the men were in the field and the telephone party line was busy.

"Get off the line. My house is on fire!" Herta screamed. Her mother came running. Herta used the only vehicle at her disposal, her son's tricycle, and biked to the field to get the men.

Arthur stood on the roof, Heinz on the ladder, while Herta handed them pails of water. My aunt held the children. The fire was quashed.

On this, my first visit in 1946, Herta and Arthur had graduated to a small one-bedroom apartment in the city. He was doing well, the horse business was booming. However, on this historical occasion of my visit they and their two boys stayed with me on the farm. Herta and I were assigned to one bed in the master bedroom. My aunt slept in the other. My Uncle Arthur and the children shared the guest room. When it was time to retire my aunt lighted a candle and started walking up the stairs. Herta and I climbed up behind her, single file. Other than the candle I could not see a thing. I was thinking of Lady Macbeth and started giggling. My aunt kept on walking and so did we. She put the candle on the night table between the two beds, flickering, eerie shadows moved on the wall. It was a scene from a Bergman picture. We all crawled into our assigned beds. My aunt said "good night," wet her index finger and killed the flame.

After washing myself with cold water in the morning I went down to the outhouse shivering. This one was only built for one. I could not help but think of their farm in Warden. One day Herta pulled me up to the bedroom. We were about ten years old. "Hurry let's watch," she said. We rushed to the window. A cow was led into a wooden enclosure. It was just big enough for her to stand in. She could not move around. Then a man led a big bull towards the cow. The bull managed to mount her but had trouble proceeding with the job. The man had to help him enter her. She stood quietly. The bull made a lot of grunting noises. He dismounted apparently satisfied and his owner led him away. Herta got a real kick out of this scene. I felt uncomfortable and was glad when it was over.

The next day we were to visit the farm in Canada. But for that evening Herta, Arthur, the children and I moved into their one bedroom apartment in Winnipeg. It had all the comforts of civilization including a full bathroom with running hot and cold water. It had a living room, which was furnished like a dining room plus a bedroom. In the bedroom were two large beds attached to each other. On the opposite wall was a bed for the boys. No couch in sight in either room. I began to wonder where I was going to sleep. Herta saw me looking around and said; "You are sleeping with us."

"Yes," Arthur said. "Ruth sleeps in the middle."

"You are crazy, I sleep on the outside next to Herta."

"No, you sleep in the middle. You are company, you sleep on the "besuchsritze" (visitor's crack)."

"No, I will not!"

"I insist."

"I will sleep in the other room on the floor. I am not going to sleep in the middle."

"Then I sleep in the middle." He said. And then the boys woke up. Herta consoled them, told Arthur to stop making an ass of himself, adding: "I sleep in the middle, basta!"

Arthur went to sleep without saying "good night." Herta was so mad she could not sleep at all. I moved as far away from both of them as I could and slept well.

The next morning all was forgiven. We drove to Arthur's horse farm. Again he saluted every horse we passed. When we came to the farm he spoke to each horse individually. It seemed to make them happy. He was the original horse whisperer.

For my last day we returned to the farm. My aunt gave me a big home smoked breast of beef to take to New York. The customs officer took it away from me. "You cannot import meat."

Two years later, my daughter Ellen and I went for a visit to Winnipeg. Ellen had such a good time, she did not want to go home.

When the first bar mitzvah came around, Ernst, Ellen, and I all flew to Winnipeg. By then my uncle's family also lived in the city. Herta had another little boy. The five of them lived in a beautiful house big enough to accommodate the three of us.

Herta and Arthur came to New York a few times to visit us and we continued to attend their bar mitzvahs. When my uncle died, I flew to Winnipeg for the funeral. A few years later, Arthur developed a brain tumor and died during the operation and I flew to his funeral. When my aunt started ailing I rushed to visit her one more time. But I did not want to go to her funeral too. And I didn't.

BACK TO SCHOOL 1949

"I think I can support the family now," Ernst said one day, after work. "Give up your job at Oomphies and stay home with Ellen.

That was a tempting offer. But I did not run to the office the next morning to inform them about my impending retirement. I did have some trepidation. I liked my job. I had been with the company for six years, had worked myself up through the ranks, had a nice salary, and even nicer Christmas bonuses, liked the people and they liked me. On the other hand it was time to get rid of the babysitter. Ellen was nine years old and someone had to be in the house when she came home from school. I decided to quit working. I did however have an ulterior motive. I would be able to take a course in psychology at the New School.

When I informed my bosses of my decision they and my co-workers did not want to believe me.

"Are you having a baby?"

Even after I explained my reasons and assured them that I was not pregnant, their answer was "Well, we'll see you in nine months." They didn't make it easy for me to leave, and the big party they arranged for my last day did not help either. I could not picture myself without Oomphies, and I had absolutely no idea how my day would look from now on. However, of all the decisions I had to make in my life, this turned out to be one of the smartest. I signed up for one course in psychology as an auditing student at the New School. I had read some of Freud's basic books like Introduction to Psychoanalysis and Dream Interpretation and to confuse myself I had also read Karen Horney.

I was scared to go to my first class. Most of all I was afraid that my English would be insufficient. While it was good enough for my Oomphie job, the esoteric language I expected in college could be something entirely different.

The class was given in the morning so I could be home when Ellen came back from school. I don't remember the course name but I do remember that I really looked forward to the classes. And I did the reading. I never said a word in class and did not relate much to the other students either. At the end of the term a classmate asked me whether I took the course for credit. "No," I said. "Why do you ask?"

"Do you know the school gives a Certificate of Achievement? If you take four courses each term, two for credit and two as an auditor you are entitled to it."

So I made inquiries about it. I only had to take twelve courses, six for credit to get this certificate. I signed up for it hesitantly. Now I would have to write a paper and maybe also take an exam. That was very scary! However, I felt I had to give it a try. Little did I know then that a Certificate of Achievement in practical terms was worth nothing — zilch! But my studies became serious and the real work began.

My first course for credit was with Dr. Ashley Montague. He was a social anthropologist. I was thrilled; it was all so new to me. When he mentioned *couvade*, which is a practice among primitive people, in which the men, once their wives start having labor pains, lie down and experience pain too, I decided to write a paper on this strange custom. I got a B, which encouraged me.

During this class, I talked a little more to the other students.

"Are you going for a degree?" one asked me.

"No, I'm going to get a Certificate of Achievement," I answered rather proudly.

"If you take this course for credit why don't you go for a degree? You can always drop out."

That made sense to me. I went home and dug out my Abitur diploma and marveled at the wisdom of my mother who made me take this precious piece of paper along. I did not know how precious it really was until I registered and found out that I would get seventy credits for it. But I also had to register for three courses for no credit to make up for my missing American education: American History, English Literature, and Writing. American history was totally new to me. All I had learned about America was that Columbus had discovered it, that the Empire State Building was the tallest building in the world and that Washington was its first President.

I learned in Berlin that the U.S. was a refuge for people, mostly young men, who had troubles or made trouble, who did not want to work or could not hold a job; they were shipped by their families to the New World to fend for themselves. I knew someone who was sent to New York. His name was Hans. He had a job in Berlin. He also had money. He only worked when it fitted into his playboy schedule. He stayed a year in New York. The only change I noticed was in his name. Instead of Hans, he called himself John. I also knew that if a man did not want to marry the woman who expected his out of wedlock child, he would flee to America never to be heard from again. That was all the information I had about America.

I picked a course on Shakespeare to take care of my deficiency in English literature. Shakespeare was not new to me because of the year spent on Shakespeare in my boarding school. Our teacher was an ardent admirer of Shakespeare and had been able to transfer his admiration to us. Of course we read the plays in German, and he is the teacher who made that strange remark: "The Schlegel Tieck translation is better than the original."

However, in my writing class I really struggled. We were asked to write a description, film criticism or something autobiographical, not more than two pages. I could handle that. I once wrote about my emigration. The teacher made me read it in class. I was embarrassed but also felt good and encouraged. Writing term papers was the hardest thing for me in this ambitious undertaking. The research, the footnotes, quotations, and bibliographies — it was really painful and I dreaded it.

As I became savvier about the courses, I sometimes took three in one semester if I could find one that did not require much work.

One of them was an elective in Russian Literature with a Mr. Tartak. His classes were better than a movie. He would act out scenes from "War and Peace" that had everybody spellbound. Besides he only gave an oral test on the books we had to read. Reading Tolstoy or later Dostoevsky was no hardship. I managed to get an A in his class.

In one of my psychology classes I had met Carole who had the same major and the same goal I did. Carole lived not far from me and had a Volkswagen. Since we attended many of the same classes she frequently picked me up and drove me home from school. Carole would not waste time looking for a parking space.

"You'll get a ticket, there is a hydrant," I would scream.

"If I get a ticket I am still ahead of the game. I parked so many times illegally without a ticket it's still cheaper than a parking lot."

Once I called her in desperation. We had to read an article for one of our Psychology classes. I had read it six times and still did not understand what it was about.

"Don't worry, I don't understand it either. It has nothing to do with your English. The man just can't write." She would also help me with my papers when I had trouble with the language. Besides, Carole was just fun to be with and we became friends.

At a snail's pace, I crawled toward my B.A. The last hurdle to overcome was a thesis. I wrote about the sexual behavior of teenagers, which was considerably different at that time than it is now. Dr. Kaback, my adviser and Carole's, who had been supportive of us throughout the years, said one day, "In psychology you need at least a master's degree to work in the field." This was true. I just did not want to hear about it then. It had taken me seven years to crawl this far.

In 1957 we had two graduations in the family. My daughter Ellen graduated from High School and I graduated from college. We attended each other's ceremonies. I met Mr. Tartak in the crowd and introduced him to Ellen. With his usual charm he said, "I hope the next generation will come to this school too." I had my degree and was proud of it. I had loved going to school. I could not picture myself without it. Remembering what Dr. Kaback had told us, Carole and I decided to go for a Master's degree. We also decided to go to a different school. A change would be good for us, a new experience. We registered at City College. It was a big disappointment. We hated the students all of whom were teachers taking the courses only to be upgraded at work, and Dr. Kelly the teacher treated us like third graders. Shaking her finger she said: "Missing one class without an excuse is okay, the second time you have to bring a written legitimate excuse, the third time you are out with or without an excuse." I was advised to take a course in Remedial reading at City College.

"Remedial reading with my accent?"

"It does not matter, we need mature people to teach it." In fact, I liked my remedial reading teacher and she liked me. A few years later she was instrumental in getting me my first professional job. We finished the semester at City and returned to the New School. It was like coming home. Two years later I got my M.A., without Carole. She had changed her major to sociology and did not graduate with me.

My family and some friends came to my graduation. For one day I was proud as a peacock strutting around with my hard earned degree. But that good feeling did not last. I was not the only one who had an M.A. I was nothing special. I came back to earth and began looking for a job.

DRIVING WITH ERNST

When I turned eighteen I informed my parents that I wanted to take driving lessons. My mother was not enthusiastic about this idea but my father agreed with me, which was important because he had to pay for them. I passed the theoretical and practical tests without difficulty and became the proud owner of the first driver's license in the family. I began to fantasize about a pilot's license. If it was so easy to learn how to drive, it could not be much harder to learn how to fly! However, this pipedream never became a reality.

At first I did not know what to do with my license. We had a car, a big Buick in which my father was driven to and from his business every day. During the day it stayed in the parking lot downtown and was not available to me. I managed to get the Buick one Saturday and drove to my hangout *Zuntz*. I did not tell my friends at the café that I had come by car, I was afraid they would ask me for a ride and I was not quite ready to show off my new skill.

The following Sunday I convinced my parents to go out for dinner. I drove them to a restaurant in one of the suburbs of Berlin. In front of the building was a football-field-size square. One car was parked on it. For some unexplainable reason I wanted to park next to that car, kind of parallel to it. I tried and tried but I could not manage it. Disgusted, I finally drove to the other end of this huge space and left it there.

Here in New York Kurt, my brother-in-law was the first to buy an old car, so I guess sibling rivalry forced Ernst to get his driver's license and buy a car too. So that's how we came by our old Dodge. We figured if the car broke down, Kurt would fix it. And he did more than once. I could hardly wait to get my hands on the wheel and get my learner's permit. Ernst volunteered to practice driving with me. What a mistake that was!

"Watch that car!"

"In a curve you step on the gas, not on the brakes!"

"You told me that before, I know it."

"Watch it, there is a red light coming!"

"I'm not colorblind. Stop screaming at me!" Every time we got out of the car we were on not-talking terms. Finally I had enough of this torture and asked my cousin Lutz to drive with me. Lutz turned out to be a good and patient teacher. I passed the test on the first try.

I became the Sunday driver. Once, after a night of rain, we drove with friends to the beach. Ernst sat next to me. It was a two-lane road. A big truck was coming from the opposite direction. I drove all the way over to the right through a big puddle to avoid the truck.

"Did you have to drive through the puddle?"

"No, I could have hit the truck." That shut him up.

However, his confidence in my driving grew. When we went on longer trips and I was at the wheel he would sleep in the backseat. I could never sleep when he drove. I always sat in front watching him and pushing my right foot down when I thought he should use the brakes.

"You don't have to step on the brakes, I can do it alone."

Once while he was sleeping I landed in Boston instead of Providence. I woke him up. "We are in Boston."

"Why, did you miss the sign?"

"I don't know, I guess I did. If you wouldn't sleep all the time you could have seen it."

"Let me drive and you can read the signs." We asked a policeman for directions but ended in the same spot, and asked the same policeman again and repeated the performance. On the third try we made it to Providence.

One summer we flew to Colorado and rented a car there. As usual Ernst was sound asleep in the backseat. I was driving on a winding road up a mountain. Suddenly I saw to my horror that the gas indicator was on "E."

"Ernst we ran out of gas!" I screamed. He just shook his head, took the wheel, and coasted down the mountain to the next gas station. On the same trip we drove on a road framed by ditches. At regular intervals the ditch was filled in just wide enough for a car to drive off the road. We went over one of these makeshift bridges to eat lunch. After lunch it was Ernst's turn to drive. He made a nice U-turn and then went straight into the ditch. I did not say a word and just thought, "Thank God I did not do that!" Meekly I asked, "How are we getting out of here?"

I had hardly finished my sentence when a station wagon stopped, four men jumped out, collected big rocks, put them under the car and said "Jump in and drive!" Ernst did get it back on the road. By the time he got out of the car, the men and the station wagon had disappeared. We could not even thank them.

However, I never let Ernst forget, that he, the good experienced driver — and he was a good driver if a little on the wild side — had managed, totally sober, to drive into a ditch.

I once got a speeding ticket on the way to Montauk. Ernst couldn't say much because he not only got a ticket on the same road the year before but we had to go to the police station because he was driving 80 in a 55 mile zone. I had to bail him out. Luckily I had thirty dollars, because he was not allowed to pay his own bail.

And then there was the incident when he wanted to start a fistfight with a driver who had cut him off several times. This was on Queens Boulevard during the morning rush hour. We had rented a little house with friends in Point Lookout and the four of us were on our way to work in Manhattan. We stopped at a red light. Ernst said "I'll get the bastard," opened his car door and wanted to get out. I was holding on to his arm, screaming, "You are crazy, that man might have a knife in his pocket!" But he kept on pulling and suddenly I just held his sleeve in my hand. Ralph in the back came to my rescue. He got up and with all his weight pushed Ernst back into the seat and closed the door. The cars behind us started honking and the light was changing. "The light is green, let's go!" I yelled.

My last and favorite story however is this one: With friends who lived in our building we drove to Jones Beach one Sunday night, to watch a show there. It was late when we drove home and a long trip. We then lived on Dongan Place near 200th Street. Ernst drove like a maniac. The streets were empty. First he just drove through the yellow lights. We did not say anything. Then he drove through a red light. We quietly said, "Ernst, the light was red."

"Just a little bit."

"Ernst, that light was red too!" He did not care. He drove through one red light after the other. Sometimes he hit a green one and we relaxed for a minute. I don't know why he was in such a hurry. I guess he thought that when the streets are deserted and it is late and dark, all rules are off. We got to our corner on Dongan Place in record time. He had to make a right turn to get to our building. The light was red. It was the last turn he had to make and he made it again as before at red. To everyone's surprise a police car was standing in front of our building waiting for us.

"Let me see your license," were the next words that I heard. I was tempted to say, "Why do you stop him now, he went through all the other red lights and nobody stopped him?" But I restrained myself. In a whisper Ernst said, "You all go up, I'll handle this alone." He did, with a ten-dollar bill.

WHO IS NEXT? 1994

I am walking north on 9th Avenue towards 62nd Street. I see the big building under construction on Broadway and 67th Street. It is taller than anything around it. It reminds me of an accusing index finger pointing towards the sky — threatening. Hilde will say, "How New York is changing every time I come." Hilde, Hilde is dead. In April it will have been four years. This is April, April 22nd, the day she died in 1990. What is going on?

I have an eerie feeling. For a few seconds she was alive in my head when I saw the monstrous construction. Is she contacting me? No, that's ridiculous. I don't believe in the supernatural. But it is uncanny. I have not forgotten you, Hilde. Hilde's son, Wilhelm was just in New York, and stayed with me. We talked a lot about you. He read the piece I wrote about you and took a copy home. And Brigitte comes this weekend, everyone is fine.

My brain keeps running like a tape.

Hilde died in April; Ernst died the same year in November. He had a heart condition and senile dementia.

I see myself sitting in the hospital.

I am trying to get some food into him.

I am the nurse for one shift. I stay till the night nurse comes. He hardly eats anything, gets weaker every day. Still I hope to get him home for Thanksgiving. Instead he dies the day before — while I sit there — helplessly watching the last quiver of his toes — and then he exhales — it's over. It is a peaceful transition — I am grateful for that — no pain, no fighting.

The tape is running in my brain. I can't find the "off" button.

Three weeks after Ernst's death, Eva's husband Gene is dead. Heart attack. He had a heart condition and dies in his own bed, Eva lying next to him.

And then Fred, Trudy's husband, after a long stay in the hospital, just fades away. Two weeks after Gene. Three men are gone within five weeks.

I don't want to think about all the dying, but I can't find the button to turn it off!

Ruth-Vera, Kurt's wife, two years ago — ovarian cancer. I hear the diagnosis. I hide my shock. She gets chemotherapy.

I visit her and she opens the door, wearing a horrible wig. I hardly recognize her. It's the last time I'll see her. If she had only gone to a doctor in New York after her hysterectomy — if! It does not help much now. Things happen so fast and even if they don't happen fast — the shock is the same.

The tape rolls and rolls.

I answer the phone a year ago, April of 1993. It's Monday, 11 a.m. Trudy's lawyer is on the line. "I have bad news — Trudy is dead."

"Trudy is dead! What happened?"

"The police called me at 6 a.m. She jumped out the window at 2 a.m."

"She jumped out the window, I can't believe it. I spoke to her last night, I had dinner with her Saturday night."

Her cancer had come back; she was supposed to start chemotherapy that week.

"I am not going to get bald," she had said a while back. I did not take it seriously. But I did not expect this — never. I still feel guilty — but I don't know what I could have done. Tuesday my cousin Ilse calls at 5:30 a.m.

"Rudy just died."

"What?"

"He had a heart attack. I called 911 but they could not save him. The police are still here."

"I'll be right over."

I go to her house. The body lies covered on the floor. Two policemen are waiting with us for the funeral home to come.

Who will be number three? It was three the last time. I become superstitious — I am superstitious. I always say "airplane crashes come frequently in threes." I am seriously worried — who will be the third one this time?

Meanwhile I call my daughter two days in a row to give her the sad news. Three days later I call her again for a different reason.

"Mum, not again!"

"No, all is well here."

"Mum, my cat died, Bandita, she was sick when you were here."

"Thank God," I say. "She is number three!"

My daughter had the cat for fifteen years, she is a real loss to her, and I am sorry but I am relieved. Now I can relax.

But the tape is still running.

Eva died last week, on Monday, heart attack. Not even her family knew that she had a heart condition. All weekend I get no answer when I try to call her. I am uneasy — it's not her style to leave for the weekend suddenly. During the day on Monday, again no answer. She might be at work but I have an uncomfortable feeling, why can't I make contact with her? I am angry. "Why doesn't she have an answering machine?"

Monday night I try again. The line is busy — good, I thought it means she is at home — she is a big talker on the phone. Half an hour later her daughter calls me with the sad news.

Guilt again; I should have told her to see her doctor, ten days earlier when she did not feel well. Should have — if — would have — it does not help much now — not much at all.

I am not waiting for someone else to die. If it is only one, my superstition claims it should remain one, at least for a while. I am glad that I am in better control of my superstitions. That does not stop me, however, from mulling over all the dying, one friend after another dropping off like over-ripe peaches from a tree. It is sometimes lonely. Who will be next? I am still hanging there, trying to hide in the shade, trying not to get too ripe too fast. Let the still-green fruits catch up with me first. Besides, I want to see that monster building when it is finished.

DANCING

On April 13th, 1995, the sports pages of the *New York Times* reported, "Ballroom dancing has gained professional status with the International Olympic Committee. Yes, Fred and Ginger, ballroom dancing is now a sport." Ballroom dancing a sport? Ernst would have gotten a kick out of that.

In my early teens I did fantasize about participating in the Olympics. No girl could beat me in the hundred-meter dash during my school years. However, once I left school these dreams evaporated fast. In every way we lived on an island in that boarding school. Not only didn't we know anything about world-class runners: more importantly, we did not know about the seriousness of the political situation in Germany in 1933.

All my life I liked to dance. When I was three years old, I danced for our neighbors and was paid for my performance with a fresh egg.

I still don't understand why I didn't get dancing lessons. When I was six years old my parents made me dance solo when they had company. I enjoyed it, though I doubt whether the guests did. I never had to play the piano for company, and I did have piano lessons. I hated them and my teacher. She made me play the scales with a pencil on the back of my hand. I still see the little round woman with her short grayish-black hair sitting next to me on the grand piano in our living room — counting. But I could always dance and loved it. I still do. I don't go dancing anymore. But I adore the ballet.

My piano lessons ended when I entered boarding school, but it was not the end of my dancing. Though it was not on the curriculum, we did arrange Saturday night dances, particularly in the winter. In the summer the big hotels on the island had afternoon tea dances. My boyfriend Hans and I and another couple would walk to the village to the Strand Hotel Saturday afternoons and dance till the music stopped.

After graduation I was back in Berlin and met Ernst. He was an excellent dancer. In spite of Hitler, it was possible for Jews in a big city to go out. Ernst took me dancing to the roof garden of the Hotel Eden. It was an elegant place and of course it was then that I convinced my mother to buy me a new dress. It was black. I did not think it looked particularly good on me, but I wore it. I learned the finer tricks of ballroom dancing from Ernst. "Turn your head," he would say, "you must always look in the direction you move." He had won prizes dancing with Muschi, my predecessor. I learned she was blond and a very good partner. I got sick of hearing about her. She apparently had everything I didn't, like blond hair and probably beautiful dresses too. However, my dancing eventually came up to his standards. While we never tried to win any prizes, and my hair did not turn blond, at least I did not hear about Muschi anymore.

On our trip to New York on the Veendam, we danced every night. It kept us from crying about the partings and worrying about the future. The boat was an island in the middle of nowhere. Every evening we put on our finery, and danced, sliding down the well-polished floor. Occasionally Ernst would show off with his tap-dancing. He was good at that too. Long before I met him I had wanted to learn how to tap. I took one lesson, could not get the hang of it and gave up. I was envious, seeing him and angry with myself for giving up so easily. But I was proud of my new husband at the same time.

During our first years in New York, we had neither time nor inclination to dance. Later we started having parties at our house or at a friend's on Saturday nights. We had stayed in contact with two couples we had met on the boat who became friends and my cousins Gertrude and Lutz joined the group. We had a portable record player and dance records, and would take them wherever the party was held that week. There was a formula to these weekly gatherings. We had drinks, scotch or rye, prepared hors d'oeuvres with cheese, salami or herring, celery and olives. By twelve o'clock everybody got hungry again and I served a homemade pea soup. When they finished their coffee and cake, it was time to go home. That usually worked, except for one night when nobody made a move. Instead they proceeded to raid our fridge, apparently still hungry. They ate everything they could find, including the leftover parsley. It was 3 a.m. when Ernst had a brilliant idea. He took out his harmonica and played the National Anthem. They all stood up and got the message.

When my daughter was nine months old we took her along to a New Year's Eve party. Our friends had a studio apartment. The baby was parked on blankets in their bathtub. The showerhead was securely covered with a heavy towel and a shower cap. In spite of the noise we made she slept soundly into the New Year.

When Ellen graduated from High School, we took her and her boyfriend to The Tavern on the Green. We picked it not only for its beautiful location but mostly because we could dance there. When the band started playing a Viennese Waltz, our favorite dance, Ernst and I rushed to the dance floor. I wore a new white and beige two-piece dress with a brown belt. The wide skirt was flowing in a big circle around my legs. We were floating around, doing the right-one-two-three, and left-one-two-three. And I always remembered to look in the direction in which we moved. It was wonderful — until everyone else started crowding us.

After a while our Saturday night parties petered out. We did not go out of our way to dance anymore. Except on vacations. In the Caribbean the hotels always had a good band. We learned the Rumba and the Cha Cha, but our favorite was still the Waltz. We sometimes requested it. The bands could and would play it. We were often the only ones floating around and enjoyed the attention we got.

We were in Cozumel, Mexico, when Ernst started complaining about chest pains one night (later diagnosed as a heart attack). He was all right by the time we got home, but it was our cue to slow down. We still danced on future vacations, but we were not the first or last ones on the dance floor. We would Fox Trot a little, then sit down and watch. The Viennese Waltz was out for good. It was not only the heart attack that slowed us down, he also became listless and began to forget things.

And slowly dancing became a spectator sport. Sometimes when a dance tune was played on the radio, Ernst would pull me up and we stepped to the music for a minute. In the end, while I was reading, he would watch the old Fred Astaire and Ginger Rogers movies. He would watch the same films over and over. They were new for him every time. It was one of the few things he could still enjoy. "Ruth, Ruth, look at them," he would call. Then I would glance at the T.V. There they were, gliding across the floor, Ginger's skirt swinging in a circle around her legs. They both looked in the direction they moved.

FIRST PROFESSIONAL JOBS
1960-61

"Carole, I will never pass the test, my vocabulary is not good enough."

"They are not going by the test, take it!"

Mary, a friend of Carole's, worked for the New York State Employment Service. They were starting the Youth Employment Service to prevent High School kids from dropping out of school. They were looking for counselors with a Master's degree. The work would be part-time in the morning in a High School.

"Your scholastic background is very good, but we need someone with experience," I heard wherever I applied for a job. This was my chance to get experience. I took the test and got the job. At the same time my Remedial Reading teacher from City College had recommended me to the Welfare Department. The Welfare Department was starting a Remedial Reading program for its clients in the afternoon. I got that job too.

The Youth Employment Service assigned me to the High School of Commerce. But first I had to take a two-week training course. This training course turned out to be a most interesting experience for me. It was my introduction to the Civil Service. We were ten trainees. In the mornings we heard lectures on the rules and regulations of the New York State Employment Service. In the afternoons we visited different employment offices. On one of these visits I observed a man sitting at a desk reading *The New York Times,* but at a distance from the crowd standing in long lines.

Two hours later the man was still absorbed in his paper. I had watched him. He did not get up once and nobody interrupted his reading.

"What job does he have?" I asked our trainer.

"Oh, he is a specialist."

"What kind of a specialist?"

"When a client has a problem or complaint the clerk will call him for help."

"He does not do anything all day?"

"No, he has to be available at all times."

There was another way to get your pay for the least amount of effort. I had to learn how to generate jobs from the Yellow Pages. I was put into an office with experienced job solicitors. I went through the telephone book and called appropriate businesses. Shortly before lunch one of the old-timers said to me: "Don't kill yourself, you don't have to make so many calls. Nobody is going to check your output."

My main task at the High School was to produce jobs, mostly at messenger services, part-time in the afternoons. That way the boys would stay in school. I also taught them how to behave in an interview and how to dress for it. That was my job five mornings a week.

One month later I started my work at the Welfare Department: two afternoons a week, four hours each. I was assigned to an office uptown. I saw four children for an hour each on Tuesdays and four on Thursdays. They were between eight and fourteen years old. I sat with them in a tiny office trying to teach them how to read phonetically. It was heartbreaking to see them struggle. I often wished I had a funnel and could just pour the words into their heads. I bought *The Cat In The Hat,* to add pictures and make the hour a little more colorful. I bribed them with a candy bar, a different one every week. I wanted them to come back if only for the candy. It was a strenuous hour for the youngsters as well as for me. The girls had an easier time and learned faster.

My work at the High School went smoothly and was very gratifying. One day I was asked to replace a counselor in a High School on 116th Street. For one week. The following Monday I entered an old huge grey building. I had to ask several people to find my office. It was located at the end of a long hallway. I entered a large empty classroom, longer than wide with a very high ceiling. The walls were a dirty grey and in need of a paint job. The only pieces of furniture were a small desk at the opposite end of the room in front of a dirty window. There were two chairs, one in front of the desk and one next to it. A telephone and a small filing box stood on top of it. On a radiator were two telephone books. The room gave me an eerie feeling. The fact that nobody in this school knew me or knew that I was there didn't help. I put my handbag into a desk drawer and hung my jacket over the chair when the door opened. A young man walked in. He had dressed for the occasion. Only his jacket was too small, his shirt was grayish white and his ash-blond hair greasy.

"Where is Miss Jones?"

"She will not be here this week. Can I help you?"

"I am looking for a job."

"What is your name?"

"Jack Miller." I took his card out of the little filing box. "He owes me two dollars," said a little slip attached to it. "This guy is here for money and not a job," I thought. "How could she give him money?"

"What kind of a job are you looking for?"

"In a garage."

"Okay, I'll try to get you one." I picked up the Yellow Pages and called several garages in the neighborhood without success.

"Jack, I guess I can't get you a job in a garage. I might get you one in a messenger service."

"No, I want to work in a garage."

"Why don't you come back in a few days and I'll try again."

"I need a job today."

"Well, the only thing I can get you today is a messenger job."

"I don't like to run around in the city. I want to work in a garage." I began to feel uncomfortable. I remembered an incident twenty years earlier. My little daughter was sitting on the toilet seat in the bathroom. I was in the kitchen. Suddenly through the corner of my eye I saw a shadow passing in the hallway. A man was heading straight for the bedroom. I caught him just before he tried to sit down on the bed, took him by the collar, turned him around and said "This way out." He did not resist. I led him out of the apartment. It was the last time I kept the door unlocked.

Jack seemed glued to his chair. I repeated that I could get him a job as a messenger. He repeated he wanted to work in a garage. He did not move, he just sat there. I began to get scared. I wanted to get out of the room but the door was too far away and I would have to pass him to get there. We sat silently for a few very long seconds. Finally I stood up and touched his arm.

"Jack I am sorry I can't get you a job in a garage today. So you'd better leave now. I have a lot of work to do."

Slowly he got up and slowly he walked through the long room and out the door. I stood holding on to the little desk until the door closed behind him. It was the only time in my professional life that I was scared.

Two afternoons a week I took the subway uptown to the welfare office. The candy worked, the kids appeared punctually for their remedial reading lessons.

One day I heard the workers complaining about one of their colleagues.

"Why doesn't she get fired if she is absent most of the time and late if she comes?" I wondered.

"Ms. Larson, you don't understand Civil Service."

"I guess I don't."

"In the welfare department you can only get fired if you sleep with a client."

"You are kidding!"

"No, I am not. Maybe if you kill someone that might be a reason too."

After a few months uptown I was transferred to the Bronx office. Same routine, only a longer subway ride. One day one of the children assigned to me did not show up. I went to Ms. X, the head of the Bronx office. I wanted her to contact the family and inquire about the absentee. Ms. X did not pick up the phone to call the family; instead she proceeded to give me a five minute long speech. I left her office in a daze. I had no idea what she had been talking about. Was it a language problem that I could not understand her? Was my English that bad? I was desperate. I went to one of the workers and told her what had happened. She laughed. "Don't worry about it, we don't understand her either."

A few weeks later Ms. K called me. She asked me to come to her office downtown. Ms. K was the head of all welfare offices and had interviewed and hired me.

"Ms. Larson, I want to ask you something. I hope you will give me an honest answer. How do you feel about Ms. X?"

I'm not going to endanger that woman's job, I thought and said: "You know, I really have nothing to do with her. She is not my boss."

"I know that, but you must have had a chance to talk to her. You can be open with me. Whatever you say will be confidential. What is your impression of her?"

I wondered if one of the workers had told her what happened? Did Ms. K want to talk with me because I was an outsider and my job was not on the line? She seemed sincerely to want my opinion. So I told her about the experience I had with Ms. X.

"You know," she told me. "Nobody understands her. She has been in every welfare office in the city and I hear the same complaint from everyone. Whatever she says does not make sense or is not pertaining to the subject at hand. I don't know what to do. She passes every Civil Service test with flying colors. She tested herself up to this advanced position. But she can't stay on the job if she can't relate to her workers, not to mention the clients. And I cannot fire her."

"What are you going to do?"

"I will have to giver he a clerical job here in my office so I can check on her myself."

"That will be a demotion!"

"That depends on how you look at it. She will get the same salary. She passed the test and kept the appropriate job for a while."

"She will work here as a clerk and get a supervisor's salary?"

"Yes," she said throwing up her arms.

"What will the other clerks say when they find out?"

"I don't have an answer. I just hope they won't find out."

The solution came to me in a flash after I left her office. It really was simple. Someone has to get Ms. X to sleep with a client.

ADDICTS

It was my last day at work. The separation anxiety was killing me. I was abandoning these men. They trusted me. I protected them, kept them in line and occasionally got them out of isolation. Will my successor earn their trust? Why did I care? They were just heroin addicts.

I cared because I had worked with them for fourteen months in a residential facility on Edgecomb Avenue and 114th Street. They had been referred to us in lieu of prison. I saw ten of the men in a group five days a week. I liked them and respected them. The respect was mutual.

They were hypersensitive people. It was as though they had a sixth sense. They knew immediately if a person was sincere or afraid of them. One of the junior counselors found a fake three-dollar bill on his chair when he came into his group room one morning. He was devastated. He tried so hard but it was his insecurity, which the men had sensed immediately.

It was in the daily group that I learned to know and respect them. The group was their chance to let off steam. And they did so mostly in four letter words. Frequently I had to ask for a translation, which amused them and enriched my vocabulary. However, they never used vulgar language when they talked to me privately. And I never implemented my new vocabulary with them.

A colleague took over my group when I took a one-week vacation. This is what I heard the first day back:

"Don't ever let this guy take your place again!"

"What happened?"

"He talked down to us, using all those four letter words."

"Did he really think we would fall for that crap? Talking like us did not make him one of us. What a jerk!"

It was my last day.

At 9 a.m. I walked through the ward to get to my office. As usual some of the men were lined up against the wall waiting for me. Most of the time they waited with complaints.

"Henry stinks! He never takes a shower. The whole room smells of him. Please talk to him."

I did, while half the ward was listening.

One morning, one man said:

"Mrs. Larson, why don't you get yourself some boots? They really would look cute on you."

"Yea," the chorus went. But on my last day they stood silently.

I sat at my desk. I remembered my initial interview with six foot, four inch George. The office was so small that our knees nearly touched. Annoyed and angry, he had answered my questions even if defiantly.

"You don't trust me, do you?" I asked when we were finished.

"I don't trust anybody, Mrs. Larson." Had George learned to trust me?

And I remembered the hunger strike. The men had not gone for dinner or breakfast. We counselors had an emergency meeting with the director first thing in the morning.

"Hungry men are not very congenial. We have to get them down for lunch, all forty of them," said the director. Nobody knew what to do. Not only was the hunger strike a new experience for us but none of us had ever worked with addicts before. This was 1967.

After about forty-five minutes we decided that first the supervisor would go into the ward alone. Fifteen minutes later another counselor was to follow. All eyes were on me. I was a supervisor.

"Well Ruth, what do you say? You think you'll be okay?" The director asked me.

"Sure I'll be okay. Besides the men won't do anything to a woman." They all laughed.

"We know that, but do they?"

My professionalism was on the line. I got up, pulled out my key to enter the ward and said, "I am going in now." When I put the key into the lock, I heard a commotion inside. And then it was very quiet. Everyone had rushed into his room. I went into one room where six men lived. They were all lying on their beds staring at the wall.

"Tell me what happened." Silence. I pulled John, whom I knew well, off his bed and into the hall. The others followed us immediately. I was surrounded by angry men.

"They don't keep promises here," said John. "We were supposed to go out and play ball. We didn't give anybody any trouble. Why can't we do that anymore?" I didn't know what to say. They were right. The administration in Albany had closed the door on them overnight. The new rule was "No more outings." I was upset about this new rule too. How could anybody establish a trust relationship when a higher authority arbitrarily changed the rules?

After fifteen minutes another counselor joined me. The men immediately surrounded him with their complaints. I pulled John into a corner.

"Look," I said. "You know I can't do anything about these rules. But I can tell you one thing, if you don't eat you'll never get out of here." Silence.

"I promise I will report your complaints and see what can be done. But I don't promise that anything will change."

Now the crowd joined us.

"Didn't they promise?"

"I am hungry, but I am not going down to eat!"

"I'll go down with you," I said. "Just think, you might be out in a couple of months."

"Is that a promise?"

"No."

"So why should I go for lunch?"

"Because you're hungry and…"

"You're damn right about that!"

"And your record will stay clean."

Finally three men went down with me to eat. I stayed watching them gobble down their food.

The rest of the day we spent cajoling, convincing, and seducing them to go down for dinner. We counselors and the director stayed until 9 p.m. We wanted to be sure that everyone ate and things were back to normal.

Now it was my last day, 9:15 a.m., and I felt like I was abandoning them. Would they try to please my successor? Sometimes I felt they kept out of trouble to please me. I did not care whether they behaved well to do me a favor or for their own good. But I wondered whether they could stick to it without my support.

I remembered when we drove sixteen-year old Frank to Montefiore Hospital so he could visit his friend Jose. Jose had tried to run away by jumping out of a window. He'd broken both his legs. Frank had promised that he would not run away from me. Montefiore Hospital is a maze. If he wanted to shake me there I never would have been able to catch up. He did not. The driver and I brought him safely back to Edgecomb Avenue.

The next night, however, Frank jumped out the window. No broken legs for him. The guard on the floor knew whom to ask for help.

"Mrs. Larson, please come down we are going to have a riot here."

I rushed down. John, one of the leaders, was waiting for me at the door. "It's a good thing you came down, I can't handle it anymore."

"What happened?"

"They want to put Raoul into a straight jacket to bring him to the hospital. He wants to go but not in a straight jacket. Please talk to the guards and Raoul. They're crazy. He does not need a straight jacket."

I talked to them. Raoul arrived safely at the hospital without the straight jacket.

9:30 a.m. I wished the day were over. I wished the group session were over. Will they embarrass me in this last session? Like they did four months ago.

"Mrs. Larson, what shall we do about sex? We need some women around here."

"Well, I guess you will have to masturbate for the time being."

"Yeah, it would be nice if we could see some red nail polish doing it."

I had taken this job because I wanted a challenge. And I had handled the challenge the men presented. It was the constantly changing orders from Albany I could not deal with.

'9:55 a.m., relax! It's just a job,' I told myself. 'You have left other jobs before. But this is not like other jobs!'

10:00 a.m. I entered the group room. It was very quiet. No absentees. On my chair stood a big picture, painted by Paul, who took an art class in the morning. It was the skyline of New York in black and grey — morose looking. It matched my mood, as well as theirs.

"Turn it around," said John.

I did and read this:

> To a very special person.
> Thanks for all the things you've done
> for all that you have said.
> You've helped us understand and love,
> and helped us move ahead.
> Good luck.

It was signed by everyone.

I read it twice to control my emotions. The room was very quiet.

"Thank you, thank you very much," I said. "Now let's go on."

"Who will take your place? We don't want the guy we had when you were on vacation."

"I really don't know. Try not to get into trouble so you can get out of here."

"Is that a promise?"

"No, just behave!"

"We never gave you any trouble."

"No, most of the time you didn't. Just keep it up."

Throughout the rest of the day, I said goodbye to my colleagues. The psychiatrist paid me the ultimate compliment.

"We are losing our best counselor. We'll all miss you. But I'll miss you the most."

Finally it was 5 p.m. For the last time I walked through the ward to get to the elevator. "I don't trust anybody" George was waiting for me at the door, all six foot four inches of him. He put his arm around me and escorted me to the elevator.

"Take care of yourself," he said. "If you run into any trouble call us, we'll take care of business."

I looked at him and smiled.

"George, I'll call, I promise…"

"And Mrs. Larson, never try any stuff, not even pot."

"I won't. You just stay clean and behave, George!"

The elevator door opened. I stepped in. The door closed slowly behind me.

TWO PROFESSIONALS

My work with the addicts had been interesting and gratifying. I had learned a lot, not only about the life of addicts but more importantly about my ability to relate to them. It
reinforced my dream of becoming a psychotherapist. The more I
learned about this field, the more I wanted to make it my profes-
sion. Helping people was my calling. I decided to register with the
Alfred Adler Institute, with the encouragement of Dr. Papanek, a
psychiatrist and teacher at the institute. I had met her socially and
liked what she told me about Alfred Adler's social approach and
his theory of "lifestyle." I enjoyed the classes, did the required
reading and papers, and soon started working with patients under
supervision in their clinic. I finished their three year program,
and, with the help of the clinic, slowly developed a private practice.

When an additional course in marital therapy was offered, I
signed up for it and began to work with couples, married and
unmarried. It was a new challenge. If an individual comes for
therapy, you know he or she wants help. If a couple comes for
counseling, you are never sure if both want the relationship to
work or if one of them wants to "get permission" to get out of it. I
liked working with couples and believe that I was able to save some
marriages. But not all of them. Every Christmas, I still get cards
from patients I have not seen in years who keep me up to date on
their lives and tell me about their children.

Not long ago a man stopped me on the street. "Ruth, don't
you remember me?" I didn't. He explained that he had been in

therapy with me about twenty years ago and told me about his daughter, who had just been accepted at Hunter High School. It made my day. That he had recognized me after all those years was an extra bonus. It made me feel young. All that swimming must have paid off after all!

Meanwhile, Ernst had become an accomplished accountant. He had a beautiful office and two accountants and a secretary under him. We both worked hard. I sometimes saw patients till 9 p.m., and he, too, frequently worked late, particularly during the tax season. We enjoyed our work.

Did we anticipate becoming professionals when we arrived in New York in 1939? No, of course not. It had been a slow process, taking a lot of time, work and determination.

Ernst started as a bookkeeper because he could do that work at home after his operations and later took courses in accounting. I followed my interest in psychology when I was able to go back to school. Without being aware of it, we had made the right decisions. It had been an evolutionary process.

On April 1, 1967 (tax season), we moved from Inwood (the 200th Street area above Washington Heights in Manhattan) to a two bedroom apartment on Central Park West. Now Ernst could walk to his office on 57th Street, and the second bedroom became my office. Ellen had her own apartment by then. It was a big move, and we celebrated it with a party in our new home. At midnight, one of our friends made an announcement: "When the Larsons walked for the first time on Central Park West in 1939, Ernst looked at the buildings and said 'one day we will live here — He kept his promise!" We all drank to that.

It had taken us 28 years to get the second bedroom and nearly as long to become successful professionals. We had finally made it.

HILDE

I hung up the phone. Hilde dead! Dead of a heart attack., Her husband Elmar was supposed to die first, surely not Hilde. In fact, he told us every time I was in Munich, "When Ernst and I are gone, you two can spend half the year in Munich and the other half in New York."

Elmar was always ailing. Hilde pampered him and fussed over him and worried that something might happen. Nothing happened to him! It was she who dropped dead. Just five days earlier I had spoken to her, finalizing the date for our meeting that summer. At least once every year after our post-war reunion we made sure to meet. Hilde, of course was my best friend from boarding school days. She had enrolled two years after me and I was delegated to visit her in Berlin to familiarize her with the school. I met a very tall, skinny, flat-chested girl, "ironing board with buttons," we used to say behind her back. She knew it and was so embarrassed, that she got up very early to take her shower alone. But after the first week we got her to join us and we stopped our teasing.

Ernst and I planned our second trip to Europe in 1956, and I got back in touch with Hilde at last. I knew through the grapevine that she lived in Munich. I had found her address in the telephone book our first trip abroad. Her overjoyed answer came by return mail. This time we decided to stay in Munich for three days. First however we went to Berlin, our former hometown.

On our first journey back in 1955, my heart had jumped for joy every time I saw a city in shambles. Every ruin made me happy, *until we came to Berlin.* I could not recognize the city. I did not know whether I should cry or laugh — my beautiful Berlin destroyed — my parents' house a ruin. I wanted Germany to be destroyed, but my hometown in ruins and our beautiful home bombed out — my emotions were pulling me in opposite directions making me sad and glad at the same time. I should be glad but I was sad. It was a very disturbing feeling.

Everyone over forty was a Nazi in my eyes. Hilde's husband was over forty. He had been a Colonel in the German army. I knew how she felt but what about him? It was scary. Suddenly I had trepidations about this meeting. How good an idea was it after all? And then the phone rang in our hotel room. I picked it up.

"Hello?"

"Mohr?" (My nickname)

"Hilde, *Ich werd verrueckt!*" (I'll get crazy.)

"How are you? How was the trip? Did anybody bother you?"

"Everything is fine."

"Hurry up and come!"

"I'll hurry, see you tomorrow."

The next day we went to the wrong airport and missed the plane to Munich. We didn't know that Berlin now had two airports. I called Hilde to report our mishap. All she said was, "*Scheisse!*" and that sounded comfortably familiar.

On the airport visitor's platform in Munich stood two giants. Hilde was six feet tall and Elmar six feet six inches. She saw me getting off the plane and started running down, I saw her and also started running. We met in the middle of the terminal. We hugged, we laughed, we cried, oblivious of our surroundings. We were called to order by our husbands, who shepherded us into Elmar's car. That was how Ernst and I met Elmar. Much later when the men knew and also liked each other, they would look at Hilde and me sitting in a corner chatting away and exchange puzzled glances, wondering what we could possibly talk about all day.

The first evening we stayed up half the night. We not only had to catch up with our lives but we had to clear the air. We had to know where they, in particular Elmar, stood and what he did during the war and the Nazi time. He did not talk about the time before the war and we did not question him about it either. He told us that he had been an American prisoner of war, that the Americans treated him well and that he learned to speak English during that time.

Ernst had been in so-called "Protective Custody" in Berlin.

Hilde's mother was alive, her father had died, and one of her brothers had been killed in the war.

My parents and brother perished in concentration camps.

Hilde had started studying Psychology.

I was studying Psychology.

I had worked in a shoe factory; Hilde had also worked in a shoe factory.

The next day we went for a walk in the park. "Are you looking for a four leaf clover?" she asked.

"Yes."

"I do that all the time too."

It was weird, we were back on track. The twenty-year interval had disappeared in a day.

She became my guardian angel. She must have been as apprehensive about my visit as I was. Wherever we went she did the talking. Once in a while, I would point out a man of a certain age, "Do you think he was a Nazi?" I'd ask.

"I don't know — but if he was he sure would keep his mouth shut now. Don't look for them, you can't tell by looking, it will only upset you."

It was like I was looking for something to upset me.

"But they do hate us here, I mean us Americans," I said when we walked out of a store where the saleslady had just given us a lecture on the pure linen quality of bed sheets made in Germany. "The Americans mix everything with artificial fibers," she said deprecatingly. It was the second time I had heard an anti-American remark. Waiting to board our plane to Munich, I heard this complaint: "Boarding passes are ridiculous. Since when is a ticket not enough? Another American invention." It had upset me then, and it upset me now as we walked out of the elegant department store.

The next morning I could not find my pearl necklace in my little jewelry pouch. I had an emotional attachment to it. My mother had worn it every day. It consisted of very small graduated pearls and fit tightly around the neck. It was too delicate for me, and I hardly ever wore it. But I was upset and told Hilde about it.

"Don't worry, St. Anthony will find it," she said.

"St. Anthony will find it? Is he finding things for Jews too?"

"We will see." She dragged me into the first church we passed. "We have to buy a candle for St. Anthony."

"I am not buying a candle," I said. She bought the candle and I followed her to St. Anthony's shrine.

"St. Anthony, you have to find Ruth's pearl necklace. Please look for it. She is very upset."

She kept on pleading with him. I had to laugh, stepped back and was embarrassed.

"When you go back to the hotel tonight look for it." I did and found it.

The following morning they brought us to the station. "Till next year," Hilde said, as the train started moving.

We managed to meet once a year from then on, either here or over there. Sometimes with our men and frequently without them. When I came to Munich, I stayed in their house. Hilde and I would stay up half the night and with the help of a bottle of wine; try to solve the problems of the world. We tackled big problems: anti-Semitism and race relations. The wine made us think we could solve them if only someone would listen to us. Frequently her husband would interrupt us. "Don't you want to go to bed, it's three o'clock," he said half-jokingly and half-angry.

Once we spent a week in Rome where Hilde became my personal guide. She knew more about art than most art historians. And a lot about shopping too, as it turned out. We saw a beautiful red silk knit suit in a window, which we both wanted, only it was too expensive. For years, if one of us said, "What shall I wear tonight?" The answer was always, "if you had only bought that red suit."

We went into a little glove store on a side street in Rome. Two American women were paying for a dozen pairs of gloves with traveler's checks. The man gave them change in lira. "Don't you have any real money?" one of them asked in English.

"Are you crazy?" I blurted out.

Hilde pushed me whispering, "Don't start trouble!"

I was upset and embarrassed and could not stop talking about it for hours.

We went to Paris twice for a week and had a ball seeing the sights (especially with Hilde's guidance) in the morning and spending the afternoons in cafes enjoying the pastry and watching the people.

We went to London for five days.

We spent a night in Verona to hear Aida in the huge amphitheatre. That night we had to sleep in one bed because all the hotels were sold out. The bed had a tilting mattress. The toilet was in the room — not separated by a door or wall; the little sink with running cold water served as the partition. Hilde slept, but I was awake all night. The clock of the beautiful church across the square chimed every fifteen minutes. Between chimes, the telephone of the taxi stand below would ring.

The opera, however, made it all worthwhile. What a show! Hundreds of people on the huge stage, thousands in the auditorium under the stars. A procession of wild and not so wild animals marched across the stage. After the performance, we appropriately ended the evening with a drink under Juliet's balcony.

We attended our daughters' weddings. We became friends of each other's children.

The last five years as our husbands' health declined, we started meeting in a Spa, Bad Reichenhall, every summer for three weeks. In 1989 we met there for the last time. Hilde as usual was worried about Elmar's health. She never complained about anything and kept her own serious heart condition a secret. She did not tell her friends nor her family, including her son who is a physician, about it. It was and still remains a mystery to all of us.

Elmar survived Hilde by five years. After her death, I saw him once in Munich. It was a very formal visit with his housekeeper serving us tea and cake. The conversation was mostly superficial, except when we talked about the only thing we had in common:

we both missed Hilde. I was not at ease. I suddenly recalled my doubts about his political philosophy before the war — I did not want to think about that — it made me even more uncomfortable. After I finished my tea and cake, I left promising to visit him again on my next trip to Munich. I did not see Elmar again and will never find out if my doubts were justified. In August 1990, Hilde's granddaughter, Sophie got married. I was invited to the wedding and functioned as the bride's "Ersatz" grandmother. I felt then and still feel today like a member of the family. I am in close contact with her children and grandchildren and see at least one of them every year either in the States or in Germany.

SWIMMING AT THE "Y" 1994

I demoted my wool-lined raincoat last week. From now on I'll only wear it when I go across the street to the "Y" to go swimming. For the last seven years I had worn my old "Burberry" to cross that street, but lately I've been too embarrassed to put it on even for that. Originally it was kind of a natural color but it did not age well; it was spotty or worse, with big blotches that were darker or lighter than the original color and as for the cuffs, they looked just plain dirty. Having it cleaned didn't change anything. *I* knew it was clean now but people who met me didn't. Of course, I looked a sight anyway when I went swimming at 8:15 in the morning. The dirty coat, no make-up, no stockings, just my old black canvas shoes and a straw bag over my shoulder, which does not hold my bathing suit, I wear that under my coat, just my bathing cap, which does not fit properly; it's too big, a "Fairway Market" plastic bag with my panties, a white plastic bag from "Lechters," which on the way to the "Y" is empty; after I swim my wet bathing suit goes into that. There's also a grey plastic bag, of unknown origin, that says, "Have a good day." In it I carry my flip-flop rubber slippers, which I wear to the pool. I take a comb, which has lost some of its teeth, and an awful shocking-pink plastic wallet with "Ruth" written all over it, a gift from a cousin who should have known better. In it are my keys and my membership card. Actually the awful color is helpful: I find it easily in my bag.

And that's how I go swimming in any season. When it is very cold or there's snow on the street, I wear my little warm boots instead of canvas shoes and a wool scarf around my neck. On the way back, I just wear my panties under the coat. Crossing 63rd Street, I wait for the red light on the corner so I can just dash over.

Swimming is my thing, my regular exercise. I go to the "Y" at least twice a week. It's not that I am crazy about swimming; it's just the most efficient exercise for me. It only takes twenty minutes. I can go any time, which I could not do when I took an exercise class and I never sweat, which I really appreciate in the summer.

I learned to swim, without lessons, in the ocean while I was in boarding school. That's why I can't crawl. I can only do the breaststroke. It turns out that the breaststroke is the best exercise because you use most of your muscles. When I swim on my back, I only use my legs but I swim faster and people in the pool are fooled, they have a harder time passing me. I get a kick out of that.

After I swim ten round trips, I sit in the sauna for five or ten minutes and then once a week, I get a massage. The masseuse has her little cubbyhole in the locker room. She is not the best masseuse but it is convenient and better than nothing. On my massage days, I always hope and pray that I don't meet anybody, particularly in the elevator of my building. I really look a sight. My hair is a total mess. Combing it does not help. Once I reach the apartment lobby, I put my head down, look busily at the floor, making believe I have lost something. If I can't see them, they can't see me either. At least that is the theory behind this maneuver.

One day, two summers ago, I left the "Y," stumbled in front of the building, flew through the air and landed in the middle of the street. A woman came running, helped me up and said:

"Are you okay?"

"Yes, thank you."

"Do you know why you fell?"

"No."

"You see that big hook on the sidewalk, your foot got caught in it." The hook I guess was meant to hold the awning up, but didn't. It was cemented in the sidewalk waiting for someone to stumble over it. My right back and shoulder hurt, and I went to the doctor the next day.

"Your ribs are bruised but not broken. If the ribs were broken you would have less pain."

Some consolation!

I complained to the "Y" and it took them three days to take the hook out.

Swimming for me is not only a physical exercise but I realize it is also good for my mental well-being. If I am tense, swimming relaxes me and I feel more energetic the rest of the day.

Holidays interfere with my routine. Last Christmas I had not been in the pool for over a week. On December 26, I rushed over. When I entered the locker room, it was unusually quiet. I saw one woman getting dressed. That was it. I walked to the other end, the shower area, took my shower — really only a symbolic act — I had just taken a shower at home, but I didn't want the lifeguard to say: "Miss, you have to take a shower before you get into the pool."

I opened the door, which leads to a flight of stairs, which in turn leads to the pool. I walked down and the door to the pool was closed. I did not even know there was a door. A handwritten sign said: "The pool is closed for cleaning until January 2nd." The top of the door is glass and I peeked through it. There was no water in the pool and nobody was cleaning it, not a soul around. I cursed, turned around, walked up the stairs with my straw bag over my shoulder. When I came to the locker room door, I could not open it. It was suddenly locked. I started knocking with my fist against the heavy door. I knew nobody was in that area but I kept on knocking. Nothing happened. I yelled, "Hello, hello," but that did not help either. I got cold in my wet bathing suit and panicky. How am I going to get out of here? Nobody will hear me, nobody will miss me and if they do they will not look for me on these stairs. Friends will call and not know where I am. Nobody will search this hidden spot. Maybe I can break the glass on top of the pool door and climb through it. I can put a towel around my fist and break it that way. Down the stairs I went. First I tried knocking at the pool door again, I knew nobody was there but I tried it anyway. Then I looked up at the glass part of the door. To my horror, I realized it was reinforced with chicken wire.

"Oh my God, I can't get out of here." Tears came to my eyes, and I started shivering. 'What am I going to do?' I went up the stairs again, knocked at the door — nothing. I sat down in my wet bathing suit. It did not occur to me to take it off and put my coat on. I just sat there. Friends will leave message on my answering machine, and if I don't return the calls — maybe after three days they will call the police, break into the apartment. But nobody will look for me on this forlorn godforsaken stairway. I ran down again, I can't just sit here, hysterically, leaving my bag upstairs. Tears were running down my cheeks and my nose was running too. Suddenly I saw a door, which I never noticed before, it was always hidden by the open door of the pool. I turned the knob — it opened! Now my bag was up on the stairs — I was not going to close that door. I put my flip flops in the door and very carefully pressed it against them, waiting to be sure that it did not close, ran up, got my bag put the coat over the wet bathing suit and raced home.

That afternoon I reported the incident at the "Y." I was told that I was the third person to complain about this negligence. They promised to put the sign in a more appropriate place.

Since then things have gone smoothly. The wool-lined coat covers my bare legs, which improves my appearance, and I feel good about it. I feel good about something else too; I have a legitimate reason to buy myself a new raincoat.

TANGO

I walked into the kitchen. WNYC was playing a tango. I knew that tango. My feet started moving. I was dancing the tango in my LL Bean gray felt slippers and frazzled jeans. Humming along, I turned the volume up and extended the dance floor into the hall. I did not miss a beat going down two steps into the living room and up again and into the kitchen.

I knew the next one too but I needed a partner. I could not dip alone. I remembered our "indecent" dips in the Strand Hotel when I was fifteen.

I picked up my lion, J.B. He is a genuine Steiff animal with long legs but very old. Two years ago he was rejuvenated. It was an expensive operation, but worth it. He is as good as new. I held him close, his legs swinging around mine, his head leaning against my shoulder. I was leading him through the apartment. I dipped him low, careful not to lose my balance.

I thought of dancing with Ernst. He would gently press my back when he went into more complicated steps. He was a good leader. I did the same with J.B. I did not want to get nostalgic. I was enjoying myself too much. We danced until the music stopped.

Monday I called WNYC and got the name and label of the CD. Barnes and Noble did not have it in their computer. Tower did. The clerk went through the entire tango collection, but they could not find it. Did half of New York want this record? "Try one of our other stores," they advised. I gave up. This was not a matter of life and death.

Two days later I saw The American Ballet's Merry Widow. It was nostalgia week. The melodies and waltzes are irresistible to me. I hummed along until I felt my friend Selma's elbow in my ribs followed by a dirty look. I controlled myself. But every time they played and danced a waltz my feet were moving in three quarter time. Nobody could see that. Too bad the Met does not permit dancing in the aisles.

Friday, on my way to the Fairway Market, I passed the HMV record store on 72nd street. I could not resist. I had to try one more time for the tango CD. They had it in their little computer downstairs. "You'll get it upstairs." The clerk on the second floor found it in his computer too. We both walked to the tango section. They had a lot. Only he could not find the one I wanted. "It must be in the house. It is in the computer," he said. "It's probably not on the shelf yet. I'll check in the back."

He returned with four big boxes. We both looked through them. No luck. He remembered another one at the other end of the floor. I stayed on his heels. Nothing.

"Let's look at the shelf one more time," he suggested. I guess his honor was on the line. If it's in the computer it has to be here.

"There it is. It was staring me in the face all along," he said, handing me the little CD.

"Are you sure it's the right one?"

"I am," he said.

Now I have to chase down the Merry Widow CD. J.B. is waiting to dance the waltz.

FIRST TRIP BACK 1955

In 1955 we made our first trip back to Germany after the war. Ernst wanted to visit his Uncle Max. He, his non-Jewish wife Frieda and their son had survived the holocaust in Bochum, a mid-sized city in West Germany. But we would also go to Berlin, my hometown; for me that was the most important and exciting part of this journey.

My feelings about going back to Germany were mixed and confusing. I was curious and apprehensive. I did not know what to expect and how I would feel once I got there. Ernst, Ellen and I flew to Dusseldorf and from there took the train to Bochum. We saw a lot of bombed out buildings from the train. I could not get enough of them. When I noticed a big house standing untouched I said, "why didn't they bomb that too?"

In Bochum, three men in black suits, white shirts and black bowties greeted us in the hotel. They stood at attention, and then bowed at a ninety-degree angle. "*Guten Tag Herr Larson, gnaedige Frau, Fraulein Larson.*" It was the old German greeting, formal and servile — how bizarre! I started laughing hysterically and so did Ellen. Ernst was mad, embarrassed by our behavior.

One of the men escorted us to our palatial rooms. Before the war the hotel had been an elegant villa.

"Do you think they appropriated this beautiful house from a Jewish family?"

Ernst shrugged his shoulders. "Like they did with my parents' house in Berlin?" I asked.

"Don't think about it, you don't know who lived here before the war."

We were greeted with open arms by Uncle Max and his family. Over coffee and cake in their comfortable home, they told us again how Max had been in hiding and with Frieda's help was able to survive the war.

But what I remember most from this visit is the delicious strawberry pie Frieda baked for us. I ate two pieces and lived to regret it.

We stayed two nights in Bochum and then flew to Berlin. As much as I had enjoyed the bombed out buildings so far, I did not want Berlin to be in ruins. I wanted Berlin to be the way I remembered it. We took a taxi from the airport to our hotel and passed a lot of war ruins and a strange looking hill.

"What is that?" I asked the driver.

"That's Mount *Klamotte*."

"Mount *Klamotte*?"

"When they cleaned up the city after the war they brought all the rubble here. The Berliners called it Mount *Klamotte*." (*Klamotte* means rubble.) They had not lost their sense of humor: I had to smile, if grimly.

We reached our hotel in the Western part of the city. No rubble or ruins on the Kurfuerstendam, a wide and elegant street. Only the remains of the big church, the Gedaechtniskirche (Remembrance Church) stood, left in ruins to remind the Germans of the Second World War, a bombed out structure; illuminated at night, it became an eerie castle. The broken spires pointed toward the sky, a threatening reminder of the war. The streets were clean, traffic lights on every corner, but there was not much traffic. I crossed the wide street against the light. A policeman was waiting for me on the other side. Shaking his finger in my face, he said; "*Bei uns gehn wir nur bei gruen uebern dam!*" (In Berlin we only cross the street with the green light!) His accent was familiar and comical. I smiled and promised to watch the lights.

Except for the eerie looking church the Western part of the city seemed less destroyed, more the way I remembered it. Only the hustle and bustle of the Kurfuerstedam was missing, which made the street less familiar to me. I had mixed feelings about the destruction. I wanted Germany, including Berlin, to be destroyed, but, egotistically, I wanted my own part of the city to be intact. My intellect and emotions were wrestling, an unsettling feeling.

The next morning we went to visit the house I had lived in with my parents, Humboldtstrasse 31. The house the Nazis had confiscated, taken away from them over night and then forced them to live in a three-room apartment.

HUMBOLDTSTRASSE 31 1955

We took the number 2 bus to Bismarckplatz and then walked one block to Humboldtstrasse 31, my last address in Berlin. We wanted to show Ellen, our daughter, the house I had lived in with my parents.

But instead of a house we stood in front of a ruin. Number 31 was totally destroyed by bombs. The only thing left was the number on the gate. The house next to it appeared untouched. Humboldtstrasse was a quiet tree-lined street in a suburb of Berlin, within walking distance of the Kurfuerstendam, the center of West Berlin.

We opened the gate, stepped over the debris, and looked at the remains. For a moment I felt myself glued to the ground, I visualized the house the way I had left it and in a low voice began describing it to Ellen:

After you entered the gate you walked through a little rock garden. In spring and summer, primulas, pansies and wild violets would bloom among the stones. Then you took three steps to the front door and entered a small hall where guests hung their coats, which in turn led to the vestibule. This was furnished with heavy carved black furniture. A bench and two matching chairs were upholstered pieces on which hardly anybody ever sat. It would have been a perfect waiting room for a physician, with the guest bathroom adjoining it. On a small low table against a narrow piece of wall stood a telephone. It was mostly used by me. I used to settle down on the floor and was able to talk on the phone in privacy.

To the right was a wide staircase. One faced four white doors, always kept closed. The door to the right led into the kitchen, the next into the dining room, the third opened on the big living room, and the one on the left led into the den. In the middle of the dining room stood a big table, which was covered with a Persian rug when not in use. Four chairs surrounded it. Two additional chairs framed the big buffet against the wall. On the opposite wall was a small credenza. A big oil painting of barely recognizable cows hung over the buffet.

We ate our meals in the dining room. When I got up late I had my breakfast in the kitchen, talking to Grete, our cook and maid. I liked that.

Dinner was served at 6:30 p.m. sharp. More than once I ran home from the bus to be on time. Friday nights my mother lit the two candles, which in their silver candlesticks, made the evening festive. My father cut the challa, which was waiting for him under a red velvet cover. He gave each of us a piece of the delicious bread. Then he poured the wine for all of us. On other days, he was the only one who had a drink. After dinner my parents moved to the living room, which was connected to the dining room by a sliding glass door and my father had his after dinner cognac and cigar.

While the dining room faced the street, the living room looked out into the garden in the back and led to a covered terrace. In summer, breakfast and dinner were served on the terrace, to the annoyance of the maid.

The living room had a floor-to-ceiling window. Big plants stood on a tile table in front of it. In a corner was the grand piano, which nobody ever played. I had stopped my piano lessons when I left for boarding school. On the walls in these rooms hung oil paintings, mostly landscapes, which my father had bought from contemporary German artists. The floors were covered with Persian rugs. Some of these pictures hang on my walls today and some of the rugs lie on my floors.

I remember one evening when Ernst was sitting with us after dinner in the living room. He informed my parents that he would leave Germany soon and that I planned to follow him so we could get married. Then Ernst addressed my father, "And what are your plans? You cannot stay in Germany either." My father did not say a word. Instead he stood up and silently left the room.

Another sliding door led from the living room into the den. It was the darkest room. The window faced the covered terrace. The furniture was dark carved wood, including the big bookcase with its glass door. It was the least used room. On Sundays my father would read the paper and smoke his cigar in there, and my brother Bert, would read the encyclopedia. He was looking for interesting information. He went to the American School in Berlin to learn English. He never had a chance to speak that language.

While walking up the wide staircase to reach the sleeping areas on the second floor, you faced a large painting of a scantily dressed young woman. She is combing her long blond hair, which only partly cover her breasts. A dark haired young man stands behind her holding a mirror. It is a copy of a picture by Tiziano Vecellio, "La Jeune Fille au Mirroir."

Two years ago in the Louvre in Paris, I suddenly let out a shriek. There was the original of our picture. I had never seen it in the museum or a copy of it anywhere. I stood for a long time in front of it — while I was slowly walking up the stairs again. I rushed to the museum shop looking for a print. All I could find was a miserable postcard, which barely had any resemblance to it. I bought it.

Upstairs there were again five white doors. They were also always closed. My father insisted on closed doors. To the right was my room. The window went to the street. Except for the couch, which I had to open every night to make my bed and a little table surrounded by three upholstered stools, everything was built in. All the wood was black and the walls were pale yellow. In one corner was an open bookshelf. Next to it was a closet with three black doors. Behind one door were the sweaters and lingerie. Behind the second hung dresses and coats, and behind the third one was a sink with running hot and cold water. A small mirror was above it, and a large one inside the door.

Bert's room was next to mine. It was larger and painted in light blue. It also had running water but the sink was not hidden in a closet. Opposite our rooms was the big bathroom. The toilet was separate. My parent's bedroom with an open terrace above the covered one was opposite our rooms. A dressing room with a couch and closets was between the bathroom and their bedroom. My mother took her afternoon nap on this couch.

The use of the bath and shower had to be well coordinated. After I graduated and came home from the boarding school, I worked in my father's office. I was the first one in. I had to be on time at 8 a.m. like any other employee. The chauffeur would drive my father to work later.

My parents' bedroom faced the garden. Mine faced the street. It was well located. When I came home late they could not hear me getting into the house nor into my room. My father never found out how late at night (or early in the morning) I opened my couch. My mother knew. She also knew that I occasionally did not come home at all. To reassure her, I would call her after he had left for the office.

When I stayed away for the night, I worried that my mother would have a gall bladder attack. She did not have them frequently, but they always occurred at night. My father would call the doctor and wake me up. I would hold her hand until the physician arrived with the relieving injection.

On the third floor was the attic and a small guest room with running water. It was the fifth door that hid the steep staircase to it. While it was called the guest room, guests never slept in it. Bert had to give up his room to our aunts or grandmother and move one flight up.

The garden in the back was a big lawn surrounded by flowers. My parents never sat on the grass. They preferred the covered terrace. I preferred the open terrace on the second floor, and sometimes took a sunbath there.

Occasionally I would do gymnastics on the lawn. Once my gym teacher came with a medicine ball and we exercised with it. She took pictures of me that day, which I still have.

On the other side of the lawn was the garage and the apartment of the chauffeur and his family. The steps from the garden to the covered terrace were partly intact. We walked up a few and all we could see was more rubble.

I looked through a broken basement window — it too was filled with debris. Most of the basement had been the maid's quarters, two bedrooms and a full bathroom. In a specially built closet my father kept his wine. And there was the big laundry room with its huge tin vats and hand operated mangle. As a child I was fascinated by the mangle. When the big washday with its big washerwoman arrived every two weeks, I would rush down after school and help with folding the sheets.

That was a very long time ago.

For a moment we stood silently at the gate looking at the ruin one more time and then we walked slowly back to the bus. I swore to myself never to take the number 2 bus to Humboldtstrasse again.

However, I did not keep my vow. In 1987 we went to Berlin again. This time we wanted my granddaughter to see the city. Again we took the number 2 bus to Bismarckplatz. But this time, I could not find our street and had to ask for directions. The ruin was gone and so was the undamaged house next to it. Instead there stood a brand new row of garden apartments. The street name was the only familiar thing left. I had nothing do with it anymore. The door to Humboldtstrasse 31 was finally closed.

A GROUP OF STRANGERS 1996

I knew "Ticky-like-Vicky" would have something to say when I returned to the bus with my cherries. I was practically paranoid about Ticky, whose real name was Grace. When the group first met in Warsaw, the start of our Eastern European trip via Krakow and Prague, she said:

"I won't know that you are talking to me if you call me Grace, call me Ticky, like Vicky."

Ticky and her friend Marion were on the list of participants with a California address but they lived in Spain. How they managed to share a room on this tour was an enigma to me. Marion was a fairly heavy smoker and Ticky was a fanatical non-smoker. I once sat next to her in the hotel lobby smoking my cigarette when she turned to me and said, "Blow your smoke in the other direction, I can't stand it." Marion sat three feet away puffing on her own cigarette.

On the second night I sat next to her at dinner. We all had a glass of wine on the house, when suddenly a fresh bottle was standing in front of me. I did not touch it. Others saw the bottle. And big Joe from New Jersey called: "Ruth, please pour me a glass of wine." I did, and then someone else requested wine and I poured that also. Suddenly Ticky-like-Vicky said: "Stop pouring the wine, Ruth! Marion and I ordered it and we're paying for it."

"Why didn't you say so?" I asked.

"Oh, don't make a big fuss about it now." From then on I carefully avoided sitting next to her or being anywhere near her.

She was not really a troublemaker. (In fact, she only seemed to pick on me.) That privilege belonged to Barbara. She and her husband came from New Orleans. Their combined weight was about six hundred pounds. They looked particularly adorable when they both appeared in shorts and Mickey Mouse T-shirts one hot day in Prague. Barbara once threw a temper tantrum when her room was not close enough to the elevator in the hotel. The group leader had to go through all kinds of trouble to change it for her. Barbara walked with a cane, except after a shopping trip, which was their favored occupation, when her arms were loaded down with shopping bags and packages. Then the cane was held horizontally to the ground, presenting a danger to the environment.

"I was promised air-conditioned buses. These are not air-conditioned. I could have gone on a cheaper tour!" Telling Barbara that Poland was not the U.S did not register with her. She turned around and waddled away, furious.

Her husband's main interest was taking pictures. He always had at least two cameras hanging around his neck and when a guide was explaining something, he would stand a few feet away, taking pictures. But at least they did not give me any personal trouble; that of course was Ticky's privilege.

In Krakow we made an optional side trip to Auschwitz. Half of the group went including myself. I was not looking forward to it — I had even contemplated not going — but I felt that considering what my parents and brother had gone through it was something I had to do.

The grounds were clean and well cared for. Inside one of the buildings was the "exhibition." Behind a glass window were masses of eye glasses, hundreds maybe thousands of them; another "exhibit" also behind glass was hair, brown, blond, but mostly gray, mountains of it, and a third one was filled with shoes of all colors and sizes. It was like a museum, a cold and very eerie one. It made me shudder and I wanted to get out of it. I was afraid to see something I would recognize, but I didn't and I did not look for it either. Then we were led to the "showers," which delivered the poison gas, and the ovens, "the final solution." I looked at all of it, dry-eyed. I could not picture what went on in there and did not try to make the connection. It was, I guess, my unconscious way to protect myself — at least in public. From the car on the way back to the hotel I saw Auschwitz slowly disappear but the shoes in all sizes, the hair in all shades and the mountain of glasses stayed with me.

The next day we were on the bus from Krakow to Prague and finally reached the border. For the Czechs to put their stamps into the seventeen passports usually took no more than twenty minutes we were told. However, we had a couple from Guatemala, Renee and Louis, in the group. Apparently the border police had never come across a passport from Guatemala.

Louis flew his own airplane every month to Miami where they owned a big apartment. They came up with a new revelation of their wealth every day. His son flew a helicopter, they had a Mercedes in Guatemala and another one in Miami, not to mention the motorcycles on each side of the border. He was a manufacturer in Guatemala and bragged about the cheap labor there. Someone took him up on that, implying that cheap labor was taking advantage of poor people. Whereupon Renee went on a tirade about the differences in culture between the U.S. and their country, claiming that one could not compare the two countries in that respect. I got up and left. I had enough trouble with Ticky.

Anyway their passports delayed us for over an hour at the border. We got off the bus. As usual there were little booths with mostly ugly souvenirs but everyone was eager to get rid of their leftover Polish money and bought useless trinkets. I, however, discovered a little old woman with a babushka, hardly visible behind a very big basket full of cherries, beautiful dark red cherries. The basket had a sign on it. One kilo for the equivalent of fifty cents. Who could resist that — The problem was that one kilo is a lot of cherries. I stopped and looked longingly at the fruit. The old woman smiled at me and I smiled back. She gave me a few cherries to try. They were irresistible. With my hands I was trying to tell her that I wanted half a kilo, pointed to the sign implying that I was willing to pay the full price. A young man appeared behind her shaking his head and somehow let me know that it was one kilo or nothing.

"Okay," I said. "One kilo."

The hand held scale came into action and a cone shaped bag appeared, which could hardly hold a pound and the cherries were poured into it by the babushka woman under the watchful eye of the young man. I tried to stop her from pouring more cherries because even half a kilo was filling up the bag. But she kept piling them on.

I proceeded to walk very slowly to the bus. On my right shoulder hung my heavy handbag, which constantly threatened to slide down. In my left arm, I held the overflowing cherries like a baby, which I did not want to get close to my blouse because the cherries would leave spots. The solution was to eat them. I spit the pits carefully into my right hand not to yank the shoulder bag down. I did make it to the bus and even found a trashcan for my pits. I offered cherries all around. Everyone took a few until I came to "Ticky like Vicky." "Are they washed?" she asked.

I looked at her and everyone started laughing. "Are they washed?" I repeated. "Where do you think I washed them, in some hidden ladies' room?"

"Then no, thank you," she said.

We finally arrived in Prague. I went to the little old synagogue and Jewish cemetery. It still amazes me that both are so well preserved and visited by so many tourists, not all of them Jews. The crowd pushed me through the little building — there was not time to contemplate. Walking through the little cemetery, I marveled at the difference between Auschwitz and this peaceful little resting place.

The second day in Prague, the last day of our trip, Ticky hit the jackpot. We passed a lot of vendors in a park, most of them selling Czech crystal, which I don't particularly care for but looked at anyway. I must have gotten too close to one table when I suddenly heard a tinkle and then the very recognizable sound of breaking glass. With my shoulder bag, I had knocked down a glass bell. Miraculously, Ticky was standing next to me. "You have to pay for the bell," she said. The man behind the counter echoed her words in perfect English. The noise of the breaking glass had brought our Prague guide to my side. He proceeded to bargain in Czech. I did not have to pay the full price.

"Why doesn't she have to pay the full price?" Ticky complained.

"Because I bargained it down," the guide said.

"I still think she should have paid the full price!"

Big Joe, who towered over all of us in every direction, put his arm around me, he had been protective of me throughout the trip and said: "Ticky is crazy, you should not have paid more than half the price. That guy probably put the bell close to the edge on purpose."

I felt better. This was my last encounter with Ticky. That evening after a big farewell dinner where Barbara, the trouble maker, appeared in a beautiful and flattering dress and, charmingly, gave trinkets, which she had brought from New Orleans, to everyone. I went up to my room and started packing while I ate the last delicious cherries — unwashed.

AUSCHWITZ 1998

I thought I had put it all behind me after more than fifty years. I was so sure that I told my daughter Ellen, to check the lists in Auschwitz on her trip to Krakow this November for the names of my parents and my brother Bert. I was convinced that my parents had been shipped to Auschwitz. The last I heard from them was a letter via The Red Cross in 1942. "We are now in Warsaw. All is well."

Through an extraordinary incident, I had found out that Bert had fled to France from Brussels. It was in 1945, when Ellen was four years old. I needed a babysitter for a Saturday night. Mrs. M., a middle-aged German Jewish woman, highly recommended, stayed with her that evening. When Ernst and I came home, Mrs. M. could hardly wait to tell us the following: "While you were out, I looked at your books and found your maiden name, Ruth Berger, in one of them. I was also in Brussels before I came to the United States, and I met Mr. B. there; he said he knew you and your brother. Do you remember him?"

"Yes, I do, but I don't recall how we met, and I believe we saw him only once or twice."

"In any case," she continued, "he told me that Bert fled to France when the Germans invaded Belgium."

"Did he know what happened to him after that?"

"No, that was all he knew." I embraced her and thanked her for the good news. I was happy, and felt hopeful that I would soon see Bert again. As time passed, however, this hope slowly dissipated.

When Ellen returned from her trip to Krakow, she reported that she had not found my parents' names on any list. What she did find was: "Berthold Berger, born August 3, 1920 died August 22, 1942, in Auschwitz."

All the pictures of the concentration camps on the news rushed to my head. My brother, Bert, nothing but skin and bones, pushed into the gas chamber, his glasses now part of the big pile of eye pieces carefully saved and on display in the Auschwitz Museum. Bert knew three languages. Why didn't they use him as a translator? It had been my consolation during the war and later, too. I had always hoped he would wake up from a deep amnesia and find me. But that fantasy evaporated now, and I knew that he must have been caught in France like many others and been shipped to Auschwitz. I thought I had made peace with something I could not change. But when I heard the dates — the final proof of his fate — it all came back. All these years I had not wanted to know the details of his and my parents' deaths. It was enough to know that they died in a concentration camp.

My parents were not on any list because they were marched to the gas chambers on arrival. For the Nazis there was no reason to record the names of the "useless." Older people could not be used for slave labor.

I felt guilty again. Could I have done more to get them out? We did get Bert to Brussels but the American consul would not give him a visa. I still see him standing on the station platform in Brussels waving to us. Ernst and I were on our way to Rotterdam to catch the boat to New York. Bert stood there alone watching the train disappear.

Ellen tried to console me. "It is a closure, mom."

I am not sure. Is it a closure or the opening of a wound that never healed?

ON TIME

There they come. Three in a row like elephants in a circus, the trunks hold on to the tails in front of them. They cannot be separated. I am talking about busses. I waited for over ten minutes for the 104 bus and now I had three to chose from. The problem is the drivers are unpredictable. Sometimes they behave like elephants. The first one goes through a red light and the other two follow. They don't care if they block traffic. At other times, usually when I am sitting in the first bus, the first one picks up all the passengers and the second and third one pass it, and I end up in the last one. So I try to outsmart the drivers and guess which one will get to my destination first. Usually the odds are against me. Either way I arrive on time and that is my real problem. I am always on time and it bothers me. Most people are late sometimes — I mean a few minutes late — I can't manage to do that, although I've tried.

I leave the house late and the bus is waiting for me on the corner and just zooms through the park and I am on time again. When I have to meet someone during rush hour, hoping this time I will be a few minutes late, the rush hour on that particular day is "out to lunch." However, the next day when I don't have to meet anyone, but take the same trip at the same time, it is gridlock all the way. I cannot figure it out.

Of course I have been late for appointments but it is always due to circumstances totally beyond my control. I mean, a higher power seems to have a hand in it. Like the time I was to give one class at Hunter College at 68th Street, across town. It takes ten minutes from my house to go by bus through Central Park to Lexington Avenue. I leave early to talk to the professor who invited me before the class. The bus is crowded in front. I stand in the back holding on to a pole. Suddenly the driver jumps on the brakes. The lucky people in front fall on top of each other. I fall flat on the floor. My pantyhose are torn and blood runs down my leg. It does not hurt but it looks very gory. It is not exactly the way I want to present myself.

One car coming from the opposite direction tried to pass another, and was driving west in the eastbound lane aiming for a head-on collision with my bus. Thanks to our driver there was no crash. But I looked a mess and had to walk the rest of the way. I was late. I gave my class but I did take a cab home.

My friends all know that I am on time. When for some unforeseen reason I am late, they worry about me. And if they worry about me, I get into a state of high anxiety myself. I don't want to be late, I know they worry, ergo it becomes a very upsetting situation. Like the time I had a lunch date with a friend on Madison Avenue at 12:30. It takes five minutes to get through the park but only if a bus comes. No bus in sight. Twenty people waiting at the stop. I look for a taxi, all have their lights off, not available. It is 12:30 already. In desperation, I start walking through the transverse, the road running through the park. A lot of cars pass me but no bus. The walk takes longer than I anticipated — I get to the restaurant half an hour late. My friend is not there. I walk on Madison Avenue thinking maybe we were supposed to meet in another place. In the middle of the block I meet her. She is just as upset as I am and about to check all local hospitals or call the police! We calm down and go for lunch. She is also the friend I travel with frequently. We always get into an argument about when to leave for the airport. She wants to get there at boarding time. Not me! If I am not at the airport an hour before departure, even for a domestic flight, I am very unhappy. After all, anything can happen on the way to Kennedy or La Guardia and once it did. The motor of my cab conked out on Grand Central Parkway.

"How do I get another taxi on Grand Central Parkway?" I screamed at the driver; after this question, unprintable language flowed non-stop out of my mouth. While I was cursing away, the driver fixed the car, and I made it on time.

Why is it that I have to be obsessively punctual? At times it is embarrassing. Nobody will stop loving me because I am five minutes late. It has been suggested that this is a typically German trait. Germans are always punctual. I don't want to have a typically German trait! As far as I am concerned my being on time has nothing to do with the Germans!

I think it has more to do with the fact that I can't tolerate lateness myself. I can wait five minutes without much trouble but if I have to wait longer I work myself into a seething rage. It's upsetting, because when the person arrives, happily apologizing for being late, I have to take a deep breath and say; "It's all right, I'm glad you made it."

Actually if someone is habitually late, I consider that insulting. If they can be on time for professional appointments, why can't they be on time for me? I guess I expect too much. The fact is that my being obsessively on time is my problem, not theirs. I just had to get it off my chest.

THE MEN'S ROOM 1989

Ernst had developed senile dementia over the last eight years. This changed all aspects of our lives, particularly mine. From being an independent person I became a caretaker. My days had to be arranged around him. However, I was not ready to give up everything, in particular not our summer vacations. I called Hilde, who lived in Munich. She and her husband, Elmar, spent their summers in Bad Reichenhall, which is a resort in the south of Germany.

"Why don't you join us?"

"Great idea," I said, and decided on the spot that we would spend three weeks in this beautiful spa. For us women it was the perfect solution. Neither of us could leave our men alone anymore and it would replace our yearly rendezvous in Paris.

And so we would spend four summers in Reichenhall, a beautiful little town surrounded by mountains, close to Salzburg with its annual music festivals. All four of us would go to concerts and the opera, provided we had the proper attire. In Salzburg everything was very formal. Once we had to borrow a black bow tie, which Ernst wore with his blue suit and white shirt.

The first few years it worked out well. The most difficult thing was that my husband could not orient himself. In spite of all the years, he was unable to find the dining room or his way into the beautiful garden with its little pond (where Hilde and I counted the baby ducks every morning to see if the cat had gotten another one during the night.)

In what turned out to be our last year there, we had the same routine. Every morning after breakfast Hilde and I would meet on the same spot near the pond, sit in beach chairs and talk non-stop to catch up on the past year. There was sun or shade under old trees and the friendly waitress would serve us coffee or cold drinks. Ernst liked to take a rest after breakfast. I would call to wake him up and then go to fetch him. This worked well until I called one morning and got no answer. I ran upstairs and found the room empty. I asked at the desk whether they had seen him. The answer was negative. Hilde and I left the hotel, walking in the opposite directions to look for him. I went to the Fifth Avenue of Bad Reichenhall, a one-street mall with many benches. On one of them not far from the hotel sat my husband, smiling happily when he saw me.

"There you are, I was waiting for you." I was happy too, but I was not smiling.

One night Hilde invited me to the opera. Her husband cavalierly had given me his ticket. It was not a big sacrifice on his part. He did not care much for opera and was very hard of hearing. Only when the music was played fortissimo could he hear it. The problem was what to do with Ernst. Elmar couldn't and wouldn't babysit with him. I asked the pretty young hostess to stay with Ernst. We knew that she liked to sit at the bar.

"Erika, why don't you stay with Ernst tonight and the drinks will be on us." She was delighted. "And Erika, when he has to go to the bathroom, you have to go with him and wait outside. He will not find his way back."

"Don't worry!"

I had become an expert on locating men's rooms in the concert halls in Salzburg. I would lead him there and plant myself in front of the door. Sometimes I was lucky and Elmar had to go too and the two came out together. But I was always worried that Elmar might forget to wait or visa versa.

When we came back from the opera, Erika said, "We had a wonderful time."

Ernst's remark: "She drinks a lot."

That year we traveled from Bad Reichenhall to Berlin. The German government had invited all German Jews who had to flee under Hitler's regime to visit their hometown. Our trip to Berlin was one of these visits. The invitation included children and grand-children. Our seventeen-year-old granddaughter, Daniella, would meet us there.

We went by plane from Salzburg to Munich and from there to Berlin, with one hour between planes. I watched the carry-on lug-gage and Ernst went to the men's room. He did not come back for twenty minutes. I walked to the door marked "toilet" pulling my wheeled luggage behind me. I opened the door. No toilets in sight. Instead I found a staircase about two stories high. I stood at the bottom contemplating what to do, when I saw an elderly couple coming slowly down. He was on crutches.

"He lost his leg in the war. He can thank his Fuhrer," I thought. The woman looked at me. "Are you looking for someone?"

"Yes, my husband. I can't get up there," pointing to my wheels.

"Does he wear glasses? I saw a man upstairs looking around."

"Yes, that's him."

"I'll go up and get him for you."

"Thank you very much." (I did not feel so good about my thoughts now.)

We made the plane, met Daniella, and toured Berlin. The wall was still up.

On a bus tour to the Pergamon Museum in East Berlin, Ernst had to go to the bathroom. I went with him. In the museum the bathrooms were a family business. A woman sat at the entrance. Nobody could get in without paying her first, no matter how ur-gent it was. She directed Ernst to the right where her husband was in charge. It was a very lucrative enterprise since most tourists did not have East German Marks. They knew the exchange rate. They collected a lot of foreign currency and contributed to the East German economy. Time passed and Ernst did not return. I wor-ried that something might be wrong with him. And I worried too that the bus would leave without us. The thought of being stranded in East Berlin did not appeal to me. I saw myself running around finding transportation and standing in front of diverse men's rooms

211

waiting. I chased Daniella to the bus to hold the departure and asked the woman-cashier whether her husband could check on mine. He yelled, "Herr Larson" and then I heard, "I'm coming." He did come out after another five minutes. The bus waited.

For two days there were no major problems. Then on the third afternoon Daniella wanted to go alone to a famous department store, Kadewe. It was close to our hotel. I did not want her to go alone. She did not know a word of German and was too pretty to leave unattended. I would not have a minute's peace as long as she was gone. But if I went with her, I would also not be at ease. What a fun vacation this was turning out to be! I decided to go with her, put Ernst to sleep and told the hotel deskman not to let him leave.

The next day we went to my old neighborhood to look for the house I had lived in. It was then that we found the newly built garden apartments in its place. An eerie experience for me, which closed the books on my life in Berlin.

We decided to walk back to the hotel. It was a good distance and Ernst was soon tired. Daniella suggested we put him into a taxi, giving the driver the address of the hotel. Ernst liked the idea because he wanted to sleep. I was not comfortable but went along. The scheme worked well.

The next tour was into the Reichstag, the equivalent of the Senate in the U.S. A big building, it serves as a museum now. We were guided through the building and passed a sign Ernst could not resist, "men's room." He went in and I stood in front of the door. After ten minutes I opened the door and saw to my horror a staircase going up and down. The men's room was to the right. I went into it. Not a soul inside. There were three ways to go back. Did he go up or down the stairs? I ran to our guide.

"My husband got lost!"

"He will come back."

"No you don't understand. He will not come back. We will have to look for him."

She found a guard who had seen him wandering around. He brought him back to us.

"I thought I'd never find you again," he said.

"You were scared?"

"I did not know where you were. I thought you had left." I assured him that I would never leave without him. For the rest of the day, I held on to his hand.

Our vacation was over. Nobody was happier than I when we landed in New York. I realized then that I could not go on a trip with my husband again. He did not enjoy it. He would much rather be home and under the circumstances so would I.

BANANAS

I came home with one ripe banana. I was lucky to find one that was not squashy. The truth is I would like to buy ten at one time. In the stores they are mostly either all yellow or all green. If I buy ten yellow ones they start getting black spots in a day. If I buy them all green they will all be ripe at the same time. Either way I would have to eat ten bananas in one day. I have heard of banana diets. I don't want to go on a banana diet nor any other diet for that matter, so I buy one ripe banana for immediate use, and two that are half and half.

Years ago there was a jingle on the radio, "Don't put the bananas in the refrigerator." One day I saw my sister-in-law doing that. "Vera, don't put them into the fridge."

"Nonsense," she said. "Don't believe everything commercials tell you."

She was right. It works. The skin gets black but the fruit stays fresh.

I think there is a competitive thing going on between apples and bananas. The question is whether a banana or an apple a day keeps the doctor away. I am not taking any chances. I eat one of each every day. An elderly person like me needs her potassium so I have my daily banana. But I would never do away with the apple. Its reputation goes back to my grandmother or maybe even the Romans. Those people definitely knew what was good for them — at least my grandmother did. I just have to think of chicken soup, which doctors used to make fun of until scientists, after years of research, found out it really helps treat a cold.

I only buy green apples, Granny Smith, and eat them with the peel. The peel has most of the vitamins. I bet the banana peel has also most of the vitamins only we can't eat it. Even monkeys peel their bananas. Apples are sour and bananas are sweet, giving my taste buds a nice change. I prefer sour to sweet. I just love herring and I have pickles with my lunch nearly every day.

You might think that my fruit intake consists only of these two certifiable healthy items of produce. The fact is I like any kind of fruit. I buy clementines by the crate and eat two to four at a time.

I remember when I was about eleven years old my aunt left me alone for half an hour with a big bowl of delicious dark red cherries. I ate the cherries and put the pits into a little glass plate. Suddenly I realized that the little plate was filled to capacity with pits and there were only three cherries left, hardly visible at the bottom of the bowl. I had eaten a pound of cherries. In desperation I threw the pits out the window. I did not say a word, neither did my aunt. However, on subsequent visits, fruit was parceled out to me.

I wonder if other people have the same problem with bananas. I see women buying big bunches in one color, green or yellow. I don't know how they do it. They might have big families or might be on the above-mentioned diet, of course. Right now I have two bananas in a bowl. Both are half green and half yellow. Maybe one of them is genetically different, programmed to ripen a little faster and I won't have to go down again to buy one ripe one.

I don't know how I got into this banana predicament. I have enough things to deal with on a daily basis. Is it possible that I am going bananas?

MY CATARACT OPERATION 1993

"It's nothing, Ruth. I know so many people who had the operation, it's really no big deal," everyone told me. It's nothing for them, they don't have to risk one eye, I do. Maybe when it's all over I'll also say, "it's nothing." Meanwhile I have to decide if and when. I do. First I'm going on my East European trip and then I'll have the cataract operation. I make the arrangements before I leave so I can't cop out.

I return on July 11, a Sunday. The next day, Monday, I have to go for the blood test and cardiogram, which have to be taken within one week of the operation, scheduled for Thursday, July 15th. Monday I wake up with a sore throat. I take an extra dose of vitamin C and go for the tests armed with cough drops. No problems. My throat is still sore and I start coughing and sneezing. What is this, I think, the air conditioning, a cold, the change of climate, an allergy? I take massive doses of vitamin C. No change. I wake up Tuesday coughing and sneezing. They will never operate if I have a cold. Should I call the doctor? No, I have to get it over with. Don't cop out with a stupid cold!

I run to my drugstore. "I need the best cough medicine you have."

"Is it for you?"

"Yes."

"Take it exactly as directed!"

"I will."

Two teaspoons every four hours. My teaspoons are small. I make sure to take a little extra to make up for their smallness. I set the alarm clock. Four hours later same dose. I sleep well that night and wake up cured. A miracle cure, I say to myself, or is it a miracle drug? No sore throat, no coughing, and no sneezing. I don't understand it. But then I don't need to understand it. The cold is gone and that is all that counts!

Thursday my good cousin Ilse, who volunteered to go with me to the hospital, picks me up at seven in the morning. We have to be there at 7:30, the operation is scheduled for 9:30. I hardly have time to go to the registration desk when a woman with lots of papers comes by and says:

"Mrs. Larson, follow me."

"I am here for the operation," I say.

"I know," she says. "Just come with me to the second floor."

Like sheep we follow her.

"Sit down here until you are called."

Now we are sitting in a big waiting room. Two women sit together when we arrive. They are very busy talking, and one is trying to read the *New York Times*. They wear light blue hospital gear and green slippers.

"Are they doctors?"

"Could be," says Ilse.

"Are they patients?"

"Could be," says Ilse.

After about twenty minutes my name is called. I go to the desk and for the tenth time I have to answer the same questions: Do you take any medication? Did you have an operation recently? In case we need to call somebody who should we call? Ah, I think, there it is: "It's nothing" but there is always a possibility — one in a hundred, one in a thousand or one in whatever. I could be the one even if it is nothing.

"My cousin is right here," I say.

"We have to have her telephone number."

If they call, there will be no answer, I think.

"But she is here!"

217

"I have to fill out the form." I give her Ilse's phone number.

"Please sit down, we'll call you."

After another twenty minutes: "Mrs. Larson, please come to the desk." The clerk hands me the same light blue stuff that the two women, still sitting there, are wearing.

"Go into the locker room, take all your clothing off, including bra and panties, and put this on." She hands me a pair of pants, two tops and a pair of green slippers. "Put this on first, then the coat."

Ilse goes with me. I take everything off except my panties (let them check me) and put my things into #33. When I come out I hear a nurse telling someone, "You put it on the wrong way, go back and change." My god, I hope I put it on the right way. I did. Back to the waiting room.

The two women are still there. I try to figure out how long I will have to wait now. Not long. I am called again, and we follow the shepherd into another area. Ilse, a real trooper, sticks with me. Now I am sitting in a comfortable reclining chair, only the footrest is down. They begin to treat me like a sick person, a patient.

"Ilse," I say, "you know what? I'm getting real hungry." I have not eaten since dinner last night and also have not been allowed to have anything to drink. A nurse comes into our little cubicle. Some more stupid questions: "You are Ruth Larson?"

"Yes." I get my name bracelet.

"Which eye is it?"

"The left one."

Bang, a red sticker goes on the left side of my forehead. Now I probably look like a tipsy Indian princess with my light blue outfit, in two shades of blue, and the green slippers and the red sticker. The nurse comes in again and puts some drops into my eye. There are other people in the area and every so often I see one wheeled away in the recliner with the footrest up. The nurse comes in again — another drop into my eye.

Now the anesthetist arrives, introduces himself and wants to know if I have any allergies. He explains what he will do. The last thing he says is, "I have to give you an injection near the eye. That might hurt a little. But otherwise you will not feel anything."

I have heard about this injection, something like the dentist gives you to pull a tooth. It does hurt. Another doctor in civilian clothing appears.

"Mrs. Larson, I have to check your lungs and heart again."

"My platelets," I say.

"You do know that you have a rather high count."

"Yes, my doctor takes regular blood tests and watches it." The nurse comes in again with her eye drops.

"These are the last drops you will get. They will pick you up soon."

And they do. With the footrest now up, I am wheeled into the operation room.

"See you later, Ilse, go out for coffee."

Dr. B., my doctor, greets me with a short, "How do you feel?" I guess he wants me to know that he is really there. The anesthetist, however, is waiting for me.

"I am giving you an intravenous now. How do you feel?"

"Fine." (Stupid question.)

"Now I add something that might burn a little." I hardly feel anything.

"And now you get some good fresh air." He pushes two little tubes into my nose.

"You like fresh air, don't you, Mrs. Larson?"

"Yes, I do."

"Did you ever have such good air anywhere?" I really wish he would stop talking.

"Yes," I say.

"Where?" he asks.

"I won't tell you!" That shuts him up. And Dr. B., says, "Good for you!" That makes me feel good. He does have a sense of humor, I like that.

While this idiotic conversation goes on a nurse starts swaddling me. It feels as if she is tying me to the table. My feet and hands are free, I can move them. She puts a heavy metal ring on my left index finger. I have no idea what it is for. I guess in an emergency I could use it as a weapon. They cover my left eye again and now cover the rest of my entire face. Only the two little tubes with that wonderful fresh air stick out. The last thing I see is the clock — it's 9:40 a.m. Where is the famous injection, you forgot to give me the injection, I think.

Now the doctor starts washing the area around my eye. I hear the heart monitor, that's reassuring, it ticks regularly. He is working on my eye. I know it but don't feel anything. He talks to his assistant. I hear it but cannot understand everything. I feel pressure on my left arm, somebody seems to be taking my blood pressure. The monitor stops, but I am alive so I wriggle my feet to let them know. Bang, something drops on my belly, he calls for some instrument, again pressure on my arm, the monitor stops, I move my feet. Bang, another instrument on my belly. I just hope they don't miss and throw the thing at my head. What will they do if they get a big person whose belly is convex? What do I care? Suddenly I hear:

"If you buy it for five hundred dollars maybe I can get it." Or something like that. Now guys, you are supposed to concentrate on me, no deal making on my time, please! Bang, another instrument on my belly, pressure on my arm, no monitor, wiggle your feet, Ruth, so they know you are still alive. He asks for an instrument, bang, I must have a whole collection on my stomach. How long is this going to take? I don't feel anything but I really would like to get it over with. It must be an hour by now, I thought it would take only forty minutes. Pressure again, no monitor, I wiggle my feet. I have the routine down pat.

"Mrs. Larson, we are finished, everything is okay." The nurse unswaddles me.

"Open your right eye," the doctor says. I open it for a second and close it again. Just give me a couple of seconds, please.

"Mrs. Larson, open your right eye, please." Now I keep it open. I see the nurse next to me with the reclining chair, footrest up. "Come on down," she covers me with a little blanket.

"I lost one slipper."

"We'll get you another one."

I am wide awake now and hungry. She wheels me into the recovery room where three one-eyed people are lined up against the wall. I am number four. They look like my siblings, all dressed in light blue with both their green slippers on. A young woman asks me if I want coffee. "Yes, please, black," and I also get a blueberry muffin. Now that is really service, and I do appreciate it. My doctor comes in and reassures me again, gives me a prescription that I can fill in the hospital pharmacy. I appreciate that too. The nice coffee lady asks me if I know my locker number and if someone is here to take me home. The answer is yes to both questions.

Five minutes later Ilse appears with my clothing. We got to the elevator. It is 11:40.

"How was it?" asks Ilse.

"I didn't feel a thing. It's really nothing, no big deal." We both laugh.

VACATION IN GERMANY 1998

I stood in the lobby of the Hotel Steigenberger, looking around. It was unchanged. Only, Hilde was not there to greet me.

I had taken a risk. After nine years I had gone back to Bad Reichenhall and this hotel, alone. Alone, that was the risk. I had spent many summer vacations here with my husband Ernst, but the main attraction then had been Hilde, my best friend. For five years it had been our annual meeting place. Both our men were in poor health. This had been the perfect answer for all of us.

Bad Reichenhall is a lovely little town surrounded by the Bavarian Alps, close to the Austrian border, and a twenty-five minute drive from Salzburg and its music festival.

I had been apprehensive about this trip, no Ernst — no Hilde. They both died in 1990. But I wanted a restful vacation and knew that this hotel would be perfect for it. My chief worry was finding people I could talk to. On my way to the elevator on the first day, I ran into Lore.

"Frau Larson, welcome back," she said, embracing me. Lore is the hostess in the hotel. She arranges little trips for the guests into the beautiful mountains or to Salzburg. She had not changed much. Maybe she had gained a little weight, but she still wore her high heels and was full of pep just as I remembered her. The high heels are her trademark. She wore them climbing mountains and on cobblestone streets. I once asked her about it.

"I have to wear them, even in my house at night. My feet are misshapen, I cannot walk without them."

Well, I thought, at least one person I know is here. However, this enthusiastic welcome was all I got from Lore. She was very busy and preferred to talk to men.

I got into the elevator to go to my room. It was now Friday 2 p.m. I had left New York Thursday afternoon. A plate of fresh fruit, a small bottle of champagne on ice and a bottle of water were waiting for me in number 365. The champagne was special, a welcome back gift.

The room also offered a walk-in closet, a built-in safe and a white terry-cloth robe in the bathroom, which became my cover up. I wore it when I went to the indoor pool or to lie in the garden. The garden was really a park with its beautiful old trees, which supplied much desired shade and its big pond where pink and white water lilies showed off their blooms and lots of carp raced each other playfully.

Sunday night at dinner the couple at the next table started talking to me. She wanted to know where I lived. They came from a small town near Heidelberg. It was their 13th stay at the hotel. They were leaving on Monday, which was the next day.

Most of the guests were repeaters. The others come for a few days to attend the music festival in Salzburg. They leave around 5:30 p.m. every night, dressed in evening finery and hop into a waiting taxi to attend the opera. (It's six hundred marks for one orchestra seat, which is about four hundred dollars.) People gather outside the hotel to see the fashion show. At the other end, crowds wait in front of the Salzburg opera house to stare at the music lovers.

Monday afternoon ten of us went with Lore to an outing in Salzburg. Eight went with her in the little van, which she drove like a pro. One woman and I went in another car from the hotel. She and I decided to stay in Salzburg while the others went with Lore for coffee and a view of the mountain. My companion had been in Salzburg and to our hotel many times and proceeded to give me a sightseeing tour through the beautiful old town. We squeezed ourselves through the narrow streets. There were more people milling around than on Fifth Avenue on Christmas Eve. We complained about our driver, who in turn had complained non-stop from Reichenhall to Salzburg about the short notice she had gotten from the hotel for this ride.

My companion picked up an electric train catalogue for her husband. He uses an entire room in their house for his electric trains. We ended up in a small café she knew and had delicious coffee and cake. But we still did not know each other's names.

"My name is Ruth Larson," I finally said.

"Brandes," she answered. No first name mentioned. Now we were Frau Brandes from Hamburg and Frau Larson from New York. Walking back to the garage for our trip home, we decided to go to Salzburg again on our own. However, that trip did not materialize because the temperature kept rising. At 99 degrees Fahrenheit, it was simply too hot. Besides there was no air-conditioning anywhere in Salzburg nor in our hotel.

However we did meet every day for a walk into the woods or mountains. Then we would stop at a little café for coffee and plum cake or a cold drink. When it was too hot to walk we went to Rebers, the café in Reichenhall for our afternoon coffee with delicious "Pflaumenkuchen," where a pianist played "mostly Mozart" in the big garden next to a larger then life Mozart statue, and we could relax in the shade.

On our last day, (Frau Brandes left the same day I did) we went to Rebers again. I decided to ask Frau Brandes for her first name. First I explained the American custom of calling everybody by their first name. I remembered when I came to New York how strange it was for me to be called Ruth by people I had just met and did not know.

"Ursel," she said.

"Ruth," I answered and then we lifted our coffee cups and touched them as if they were wine glasses. But we still addressed each other with the formal "Sie." It takes longer than two weeks to be on the informal "Du."

Years back, when I had a new boyfriend in Berlin it was always a special occasion to change from the Sie to the Du. We kept addressing each other with Sie in front of our parents for weeks. The Du came with the first kiss.

I met my dinner neighbor in the lobby one morning. Even after conversing every evening that week, we still did not know each other's names.

"My name is Ruth Larson," I said.

"Zippel," she answered, "and don't laugh." (Zippel sounds funny in German.) That was on Wednesday, which was their last day. At dinner Frau Zippel suddenly said, "We lived in Poland. But we are Germans."

"When did you come to Germany?"

"In 1945. After the war all Germans left Poland. Some of our friends went to the U.S. We wanted to stay in Germany."

Then Herr Zippel, who had never addressed me before, turned to me. "You know," he said. "The Poles killed Germans too, not only Jews. Nobody talks about that!"

"Oh, I did not know that."

"Yes they killed Jews and Germans. Nobody says a word about it."

I finished my dessert a little faster than usual. Leaving the table, I wished them a good trip home and was glad that they would leave early the next morning.

The next day I asked Ursel if she knew that the Poles killed Germans the way they had killed Jews. "Never heard of it."

When Sophie came the second weekend to visit me, I asked her too. She had never heard that either. "Of course during the war they killed each other," she added.

Sophie, Hilde's granddaughter, had taken the night train from Hamburg to spend two full days with me. Her visit turned out to be the highlight of my stay in Bad Reichenhall. I had known Sophie since she was born, had attended her wedding and visited her in Hamburg after her first baby was born. That was two years ago.

I picked her up from the station early Saturday morning. She looked good with her new short haircut and was as lively as could be in spite of the long trip. She checked into the hotel and then we went shopping. Exhausted from the heat we spent the rest of the day in the garden of the hotel lounging on the mattress-covered chairs in the shade. We ordered coffee and Pflaumenkuchen, which was served to us and wallowed in the luxury.

Sophie again had questions about my emigration. We had talked about it many times before, and she knew of it from Hilde but she still wanted to hear more details. Suddenly she said, "You know, you should write that all down. I want my children to read it one day. Not only do I want them to know all about the Nazis, but, more importantly, I want them to know your story and what you had to go through to survive."

Saturday night, our only night together, we opened the little bottle of champagne for dinner and then sat with a drink in the bar to have more time together. It gave her a chance to complain about her mother who likes to visit her and the little children but will not babysit, not even for a short time. When I put her on the train Sunday night we both felt lousy.

"Can't you stay another day?" I said. It was a rhetorical question, I knew she had to go home — but I did want her to stay. It was as if I was saying, "Goodbye" to Hilde those many years ago, when we both were fighting tears — unsuccessfully.

"When I come back here next year you have to stay longer," were my parting words.

"I'll call you from Hamburg tomorrow," she shouted when the train started moving. I stood glued to the platform waving to her until she disappeared. I turned around and walked slowly back to town for my nightly constitutional on Main Street. I inspected the bookstore window closely. "Hitler and Goering," a book hiding in a corner jumped into my eyes. During the day it had been hidden behind boxes in front of the window.

The next morning Ursel and I went in and asked for the book. He gave us two books. One in English and one in German. A former SS man was the author. It was a 4th edition, 1998. It showed pictures of Hitler in Berchtesgaden, of his bunker and of the beautiful view. It had photos of Goering, Eva Braun and the author himself in his SS uniform. It talked about the jealousies between Goering and Bohrman, who both wanted to be Hitler's right hand. It left me cold. It was just a book. It wasn't anything personal. I knew there were still Nazis in Germany. While I was more sensitive to Nazi or anti-Semitic vibrations in Germany, this book had no effect on me.

However, I had quite a different experience on the first Sunday morning of this holiday. I found myself sitting in a big church in Salzburg shaking my head. What made me go into this church for the Sunday morning mass? I had expected a Mozart Mass. It was a misunderstanding on my part. I had been eager to go with Lore and a little group on an outing. I had expected a concert. Instead I was attending a Catholic service with smatterings of Mozart between the standing up and the kneeling. I stayed glued to my seat. If I had been sitting on a pile of hot coals I would have been more comfortable.

If Hilde were here she would have warned me. I would have had no need to meet people. If Hilde were here, she would have warned me. I would not have sat in this church. I would have no need to meet people. I don't even go to Synagogue and here I was attending a Catholic service — in Austria! I was thinking of walking out but did not have the guts to do it. The Austrians were worse than the Germans! But they are a different generation. And I am the one who is always offended by generalizations. Not all Germans were Nazis. Some were killed in camps. Hilde was a German, she was not a Nazi.

But sitting in this church I could not be rational. I was the only Jew in this mass of people. Was everybody staring at me? I did not look around. I was fidgety, goose pimples were crawling down my back. My eyes were hypnotized by my right foot, which was swinging back and forth. I could not control it — I did not want to control it.

I have been in many churches, to weddings, and on trips, but I had never felt like this before. Was it because they were all Austrians? They were more anti-Semitic than the Germans. I was surrounded by them.

At least I was not alone. I had met Ursel. My gut feeling about her had been positive from the first day we had spent together in Salzburg. "Do you ever talk about the war and Hitler?" I asked her one day.

"No, not really. I roughly know what went on but we never talk about it."

"Do you mind if we talk about it?"

"No, I find it very interesting. In fact, I would be glad to. I did not learn anything about the Nazi era in school. I was the first generation after the war that attended school." I suddenly realized that she was a generation younger than I, my daughter's age, and I wanted to know what her generation knew and thought about that time. I wanted to hear that the younger generation was not anti-Semitic, that things really had changed. Ursel was eager to hear my story. She had never talked to a Jewish person who lived through the Nazi era. Her distressed reaction pleased me. I felt that my gut feeling about her had been correct.

It suddenly occurred to me that every time I am with Germans we talk about the Nazi era. Even with Sophie whom I have known since she was born and who is well informed about all that went on, we end up on that subject. Maybe it is I who cannot get enough of it.

Psychology was another subject I talked about with Ursel. She worked as a volunteer in a hospital, mostly with cancer patients. The doctors liked her work and encouraged her to go back to school. And so did I. In spite of our difference in age we were compatible and we liked each other.

Ursel's husband had to undergo an operation as soon as she got home. She was not looking forward to that and continued to talk about her marriage and its problems. Her husband had retired last year at age fifty-five. He had been a successful businessman and she felt he was much too young to retire. His hobby, the electric trains, kept him busy now. Ursel is very much attached to her married son and showed me a photo of him, the only picture she carried. And she was proud of her four-month-old granddaughter.

I can still see us sitting on a shady bench in the beautiful Kurpark. It was our last day and feeling very close, we decided to exchange addresses, promising to keep in touch and even planning to meet in Bad Reichenhall again the following year.

For my last dinner I had ordered Pfefferlinge with scrambled eggs. I had to order it the night before since it was not on the menu. It is one of my favorite dishes. Pfefferlinge, small very tasty mushrooms, are hard to get in New York.

My new neighbor at dinner looked enviously at my plate and asked me about it. She was from New York and lives on East 68th Street. It was her fifth visit to the hotel. She had immigrated to New York the same year I did. Someone from home! It made me feel warm inside. We started talking about New York and where in Germany we had originally come from. She had lived in Frankfurt, I in Berlin until 1938. I was sorry that I could only spend one meal with her. It felt good to talk to someone from New York. While packing my suitcase that night, I realized that my vacation had worked out better than I had anticipated. I did find company after all and might even have started a new long distance friendship. Sophie had come, if only for two days, the best days of this holiday!

Next morning it was Ursel, not Hilde, who waited for me in the lobby. We said goodbye and then she climbed into her taxi to go to the station and I boarded mine to get to the airport in Salzburg.

TRYING TO DO MY TAXES

Sometimes it seems to me that the chair at my desk has a propellant built in. I know I have to do my taxes, I want to do my taxes, at least I think I want to, but I find a good reason to jump up every five minutes. And sometimes I can cop out before I even sit down. Today, Thursday, is such a day. I made up my mind this morning to do the dreaded task, except Thursday is my day to go swimming at the "Y." I could postpone that to Friday, except I have a massage appointment at the "Y" too and it is not fair to cancel that at the last minute. Besides swimming has a high priority in my life. Exercise keeps me young, flexible and healthy. In fact the first question my doctor asks when I come for my regular check up is: "Are you still swimming?"

But it is not only the swimming itself that delays me; there is a ritual attached to it. First when I come home I have to wash my hair and then as a reward for the exercise, I have a cup of coffee and a cigarette. By the time I get dressed my hair is dry. While I sit smoking peacefully, I realize that I have an appointment with my accountant in two days. I haven't even started to prepare for it. Should I go through my checkbook first or take my AMEX bills out? It bothers me that I can't even make that decision. I just can't get it together.

The telephone rings. Is that a welcome sound? Another excuse to avoid what I have to do? Of course it is. But it is not my fault. I did not use any ESP to get Rose to call me. In fact, she disturbs me in my thinking and I have not finished my coffee either. I could let the answering machine take the call but that is very hard particularly when you sit right next to it. Now Rose talks like a waterfall, I have a hard time stemming the tide. She literally runneth over. Besides I am not interested in her trip to the mall yesterday, where she had a good lunch but could not find one thing that she wanted to try on, and the holidays are coming, and what will people think if she does not have something new to wear, and you don't know what the weather will be. Cool enough to wear a suit or warm enough to wear a summer dress, a dark one of course. It's a real problem for Rose but not for me. Now it is my patience that runneth over. I interrupt her loud and clear and lie; "The doorbell is ringing, my handyman is here. I'll call you soon," and I hang-up. Of course that is not nice but it's only a little white lie and in self-defense they are permitted.

The result of the phone call is that my piercing and profound thoughts have been interrupted, and I suddenly realize that I have to go to the Fairway Market. I don't have a thing in the fridge. There are two important reasons that I have to go now: I can walk in the shade, after all it is twelve blocks to that market, and the store is not as crowded as in the afternoon.

But before I go I have to eat my daily yogurt, another ritual. Yogurt is my only source of calcium and calcium is particularly important for women my age, whatever that might be. The guilt is creeping up on me: I really have to do my taxes! I'll do them when I come back from my marketing trip except that I know from experience that I will be hot and tired and I have not read the Times yet, not even one headline, not to mention the Op-Ed page. Not that there really is any big news since yesterday but I have to read it, otherwise I feel incomplete. I guess this is another ritual. With all my rituals I can't do any work. Am I a compulsive person? I never thought of myself that way, but who knows? Or are they just convenient cop-outs? When I am out of town, on a trip, there is no swimming, no yogurt, no Times and the strange thing is, I do survive.

Now off to Fairway. I walk fast not to waste too much time, and I come home, as predicted, hot and tired. Now half a day is nearly gone and I have not even looked at my checkbook, and I am a morning person to boot. I force myself to sit at my desk. There lies yesterday's junk mail. I should go through it before I get today's mail, probably mostly junk too. I clear the desk. I take out my checkbook and the AMEX bills.. I sit down and look at them. It's all I can muster. My propellant chair goes into action again. I jump up, grab the Times and start reading. The guilt is a heavy load on my back — let it sit. I'll do the taxes tomorrow, or maybe tonight? Sometimes after dinner I get a second burst of adrenaline, maybe I'll have one of those bursts tonight!

DEAF 1998

Sunday March 15th, I arrived at Kennedy from my five-day
stay in San Francisco. My ears were clogged when I got off
the plane. They had been clogged when I landed in San Francisco
too. By the time we arrived at my granddaughter's house, they had
unclogged. However, when I got to my apartment in New York
my hearing was still impaired. I made one telephone call — I could
hear on the phone — to my cousin confirming our dinner appointment for the next day, Monday.

I had been fighting a cold ever since I came back from Puerto
Rico. It had not improved in San Francisco. But a little cold never
kept me from going ahead with my plans or my daily routine. My
nose was running non-stop, interrupted by a light cough. Otherwise I felt fine.

When I woke up Monday morning my hearing was unchanged.
New York seemed very quiet. I looked out the window. The traffic
was as usual, heavy, I just could not hear it. There was still a curtain or, rather, heavy drapes, over my ears. I made an appointment
with my doctor for that afternoon. I could only hear the phone
ring when I was right next to it. To my ears it did not ring, but
made a strange low buzzing sound. I was practically deaf!

On the street the cars were chasing traffic in silence. I waited
patiently for the green light on every corner. I could only understand people if they talked to me directly and looked at me. When
they spoke in a low voice, I had to ask them to repeat it. "What
did you say?" became my mantra and I explained that my hearing
was temporarily out of order. That was my hope. The doctor gave

me an antibiotic. According to him, this would take care of my bronchitis, which was his diagnosis, as well as my hearing.

"And don't swim," he said.

That evening my cousin Ilse was supposed to pick me up for our dinner date at 6:30 p.m. By 6:45 she had not arrived. I could not understand it, she was always on time. Suddenly I heard a buzz and picked up the telephone. "Your cousin is here."

"Send her up," I said and wondered why he didn't call me on the house phone. When I opened the door, Ilse's face was white. She threw her arms around me.

"Thank god, you are okay!"

I had not heard the house phone. She and the doorman had come up and rung my doorbell, knocked on the door, called me through the door. They did not get an answer. The telephone was their last resort. She did not have to tell me what she expected to find if they had had to open the door with the super's keys.

Now I carried my cordless phone in my left hand wherever I went. When I expected the handyman I sat in the kitchen where the bells for the house phone and the entrance door are located. It was the only place where I could hear their low buzz.

The week passed slowly. I took my medication. My cough got better and I needed fewer Kleenex. But my hearing was unchanged. What if it never came back? I don't hear as well as I used to anyway — and now this! I had had my ears checked six months ago. I was told that my hearing was within the normal curve. A hearing aid at this time would not help. It sure would help now. If this is not going to get any better, I will be a disabled person! I promised myself I would not complain about my sight impairment anymore if I only could hear again. I better start inquiring about hearing aids. On TV they have this commercial for an invisible little thing, no bigger than a contact lens. What a thought. They beep all the time. I hear them in concerts. Maybe soon I will be one of the beepers and everyone will turn around and stare at me.

My maternal grandmother was deaf. They were always shouting at her. She just smiled and nodded her head. Nobody knew if she heard anything. I thought she was just not very bright. She probably was as bright as anyone else but just could not hear. She was smart enough to drink a cognac every night before she went to bed. She lived in Cologne and when she came on her yearly visit to Berlin, my father put a bottle of cognac on her night table. She got a real kick out of that and laughed when she discovered it. It was the only fun she had.

Maybe I have her genes? I like cognac too. However I don't drink it every night. Not yet. What if this was the beginning?

A week passed and I still could not hear.

On Tuesday of the second week I had an appointment with an otologist. First thing he said, "Never fly with a cold!"— easier said than done — and added that I had water in my ears. His technician gave me a hearing test. The results as expected were very poor.

Then he prescribed a regimen of pills for six days. Follow the directions on the package. Six pills the first day, five the next, etc. always at particular times. I took the first two on the first day after breakfast instead of before, could that make a difference? The coming weekend I had signed up for a meeting with a group from Ethical Culture in Pawling, N.Y. The weather was beautiful and so were the walks in the sunshine. But I could not participate in any discussions. I could not hear a thing.

At dinner we were sitting eight at a table. I could not understand what the person next to me said. I had taken the medication religiously as directed but nothing changed. I was checking my ability to hear constantly. Did I hear what the person three feet away said? No. When I sat on the toilet I tried to hear the tinkle. I strained to hear it but it was no use.

I took my last pill on Sunday in Pawling. I still could not hear. It was now fifteen days since I had come back from San Francisco. Fifteen days deaf — not stone deaf — but deaf. I identified with the few people I know who are hard of hearing. I decided I would call Charlotte who must have a very good hearing aid. I know how her hearing is. However, on this weekend she had been able to follow any conversation while I was sitting there like a moron. I began to wonder if being deaf is worse than being blind.

"Stop it," I told myself.

I felt excluded from everything that went on verbally. Sometimes I would ask, "What did you say?" when everyone was laughing

Ruth Larson

at something. I had explained to everyone at the Pawling weekend what had happened to me. They were patient but it did not make me feel any better. I could not walk around for the rest of my life telling people that I lost my hearing somewhere between San Francisco and New York and assure them that I was still looking for it.

I called the otologist Monday and got an appointment for Tuesday morning. I was not looking forward to it. Somewhere along the line he had hinted as a last resort there was a painful procedure that could be done. Anything would be better, even a painful procedure, than this. Tuesday morning I woke up to a lot of noise. I heard the traffic on the street! The tinkle in the bathroom and the telephone bell sounded normal. Was it a miracle or the medication? I kept my appointment with the doctor.

"I told you not to worry. Just don't fly with a cold again."

"But what if I have to?"

"I'll give you a prescription, and take Sudafed before you go on the plane. Blow your nose with your mouth open (which is very difficult) and chew gum. And don't fly with a cold!"

"I got the message," I said.

I took another hearing test. I was back to my slightly impaired condition and dismissed.

"Good luck! And don't fly with a cold," he said, smiling at me.

THE CARVING KNIFE

I took my carving knife and cut the apple in half. It is an old knife. The handle is black wood. The blade is a dull multi-shaded grey. I washed and dried it immediately and put it back into the drawer. Then I took a small fruit knife and cut the apple into small pieces. I did not peel it.

Daniella was watching me, ready to eat the apple.

"Why did you wash the knife right away?" asked my grand-daughter.

"I brought the knife from Berlin. It's very old. If you don't wash and dry it immediately, it will get brown spots and rust.

"I will remember that." With those words the knife became an heirloom. I did buy myself a new carving knife at Macy's about fifteen years ago. It was made in the same city the old one came from, Solingen, Germany. The multi-shaded grey one is now strictly the apple-cutting-in-half knife. I really have an emotional attachment to it.

I have emotional attachments to the strangest things. There is the aluminum strainer that immigrated with me to the U.S. It's one of the few pieces that was damaged on the trip. It arrived with the handles broken off and slightly bent out of shape.

"Mom, can't you afford a new strainer?"

"I don't want a new strainer, I like this one." One day Ellen bought me a ceramic strainer. It was not good. The holes were too big, some blueberries slipped into the sink. When it broke a few years later I did not shed a tear.

And then there is the heavy purple glass vase in the shape of a goblet. It's adorned with the picture of a man courting a woman. He is offering her flowers. She is holding on to a big staff, like a shepherdess. They are standing in the shade of a big tree. It looks like a baroque shepherd's scene. The picture is daintily drawn in gold. I would like to use the vase but the only flowers that would look good in it are sweet peas. I never see those anymore. When we lived in Inwood, we had a little flower shop on Dyckman Street. George, the owner, always decorated his window seductively. It was hard for me to pass it without buying something. On a vertical stand in the window he had sweet peas in all colors, pale pink, pale blue, pale lilac, and white. I picked a bunch of lilac blooms and put them into my purple vase. I positioned the vase so you could not see the gold shepherd's scene. It looked beautiful if only for a short time. Sweet peas don't last very long. The other vase that came with me to New York is narrow and off-white. My mother had bought it on sale at Wertheim's, the biggest department store in Berlin. She had been looking for dishes, instead she came proudly home with a bargain, a vase. It looked like a bargain too. When I put flowers into it now, I try to bend a leaf down to cover the crack.

And then I have ten volumes of Shakespeare's plays. It's not a complete edition. Othello for one is missing but Hamlet, Macbeth and Romeo and Juliet are included. One page is in English and the opposite page is in German. It was a birthday present from a friend when I had to take an English Lit. course at the New School. He found the books in a second-hand store. And they look it. I am a little embarrassed to have them on my bookshelf in the living room. Richard III and Hamlet have completely lost their backs. They look crummy, but you have to crane your neck to see them. I put them on the top shelf. They are the only Shakespeare I have and I am very much attached to them. They remind me of my boarding school and our extensive study of Shakespeare.

And then I have a tiny silver forget-me-not pin. It was the last birthday gift Hilde gave me. She sent it to me in February. Two months later she died suddenly. Did she have a premonition?

Bertchen, my mother substitute and friend in America, once gave me an oversized porcelain pillbox. It is in the shape of a heart, flat and white with little red hearts painted on it. Bertchen was a baby nurse. She was in my apartment when I came home from the hospital with my baby. She watched me putting diapers on Ellen for the first time and supervised me when I gave her her first bath. She became part of the family and I want the little box to stay in the family.

And then there is the Delft tile table. We had two tables made of these beautiful tiles in Berlin. My parents shipped them both to New York for me. Each table was made with eighteen tiles. However, only twelve survived the long journey. For twenty-five years, I kept the twelve tiles carefully wrapped in a closet. When we moved to Central Park West, I had them made into a table. I put plants on it. Just like mother had done. Now I collect tiles. Wherever I travel I look for them and bring at least one home as a souvenir. I have tiles from Mexico, Greece, Austria, Germany, Italy, Spain and even China, where I had a hard time finding one. They decorate the walls of my dinette and match the kitchen table whose tiles I brought from Spain. The tiles of the coffee table in my living room come from Mexico.

Jewelry is an heirloom in itself, and I am attached to all the pieces my mother wore. There is, however, one piece she never wore, a pair of diamond earrings. They were too gaudy for her. She always wore little pearls in her pierced ears. When Ernst was in the hospital with his bad back and I didn't have enough money to pay my forty-two dollar rent, I brought the diamond earrings to a pawn shop and got my rent money. I bought them back a year later. Many years later they were transformed into a ring. It is my favorite.

After I had told Daniella the history of the carving knife, I proceeded to tell her about the other things close to my heart. She listened and said, "Don't worry, I'll remember it."

P.S. I will not hold it against her or Ellen if they get rid of the strainer or the vase with the crack.

MONTAUK

We drove to Montauk last Memorial Day weekend. It's our yearly pilgrimage to Lenhart's cottages. The sky was blue. We were in luck with the weather. However, weather never did hold us back from driving to the island, rain or shine, Montauk it was. One July 4th week, it rained for seven days. Mrs. Lenhart was desperate, some guests actually left. We stayed, drove to East Hampton looked into the stores and spent money.

And there was the day in May when we left New York under a dark grey sky. By the time we got on the two-lane road, the last stretch to Montauk, a white wall of fog hit us. The road here was and still is narrow, curvy and hilly. Ernst drove five miles an hour, kept the door open with his left hand to see the white line separating the lanes. It was scary.

I knew how dangerous fog could be. I was reminded me of the incident in Juist years before: four of us walking along the ocean strand as thick fog surrounded us, the moon gleaming eerily through the mist. Scary!

For forty-two years we went to Montauk every summer. Some years we spent our summer vacations there and some years we went just for the long weekends. We had fallen in love with the place.

It was very hot the first time we went out there. Someone had recommended East Hampton. We had never heard of the Hamptons. It seemed that half of New York had the same idea. All the hotels were filled. We had to spend that first night in an unbearably hot room on the top floor of a B&B. Early next morning we drove east toward Montauk. The few motels we passed had their "no vacancy" signs proudly displayed. We came to the Old Montauk highway, a two-lane road along the dunes with a view of the sea. My eyes were glued to the ocean. It was low tide. The beach was white and very wide and the sea blue, mirroring the sky. "Juist," I thought. Could it be that I found a place where the beach was as beautiful as the one on the island where I spent six years in school? In my mind there was no other shore like it. I knew that could not be true, but I wanted it to be true. I wanted the place where I spent my teen years to be unique. I knew the school was peerless but I wanted the beach to be the most beautiful one in the world. There I had learned to love and respect the ocean, when it was quiet and when it was rough. It was like a first romantic love. You always remember the unsurpassable beauty of it.

Suddenly Ernst stopped and ran towards a cottage where people were loading their car. "Are you leaving?"

"We had to, another party is moving in at eleven."

"Wait a minute!" someone screamed. It was Mrs. Lenhart. She came running down the dunes, waving her hands, a red scarf around her head, yelling; "Their child got sick. They just cancelled their reservation." The couple started unloading their car.

"I only rent it for the week."

"I'll take it," said Ernst. And that is how we got acquainted with Lenhart's and Montauk.

We moved into our little one bedroom house immediately and told the unhappy couple to leave their suitcases in the cabin until they wanted to leave that night.

I did not unpack. I rushed down to the beach getting my feet wet. Walking along the water that first day in Montauk, I realized that maybe I had found Juist's match. I was so happy.

The Lenharts were the original odd couple. She was four feet ten and round. She ran up and down the dunes, supervising the maid, looking after the flowers and chasing her beautiful big white cat into the house. It had been her idea to build the five units overlooking the ocean. It was she who had designed and furnished them. She had made the curtains, bedspreads and lampshades. She cut pictures from magazines and framed them herself. The curtains matched the slipcovers in the living room. It was all in good taste: rustic. The reservations were made with her and when we left we paid her. Mr. Lenhart did not get involved. He sat in front of his cottage up on the dune, beer can in one hand, cigar in the other, watching his property. His conversation consisted of complaints about politics in general and in the Hamptons in particular. When we got to know him better, he would complain about the guests to us too.

"Those people will never walk on my property again!" was his frequent threat. During the week, he had a job in New York. Friday afternoon he arrived promptly in his big Cadillac. Then he blew his horn and Mrs. Lenhart, red scarf around her head would run down to join him. They went food shopping for the week and to get a fresh supply of beer and liquor. He was the chauffeur, which was his one and only contribution to running this little show. Mrs. Lenhart could not drive and had no intention of learning.

The cabins had no phones but the Lenharts had a pay phone in their house for guests if they did not mind being overheard. They accepted calls and were dependable with messages or called you, screaming, "Ruth, telephone," from the top of the hill.

We got used to the Lenharts and their idiosyncrasies. In fact, over the years we became very friendly and frequently went up to their house after dinner for drinks and to hear the latest Montauk gossip. When we arrived for our 25th year, they invited us and another couple for dinner to the just opened and very fancy Montauk Yacht Club. When the bill came, Mr. Lenhart studied it for a long time.

"You look at it," he said to Ernst.

"They added the date to the total," Ernst said and asked for an itemized bill.

"We lost it," said the waiter. "But we will reconstruct it for you."

They had made a twenty-five dollar mistake. That was a lot of money at the time. A brandy on the house was the consolation prize.

The demand for their cottages grew. They built five more units up on the dunes and a beautiful house for themselves. They also added a small swimming pool. We had to make our reservations early, if we wanted to get number four, our favorite cottage. It has a beautiful garden and is near the pool. Mockingbirds come to feed on the big orange flowers on the shrubs growing in front of our window.

The Lenharts never sat at the pool. All week long, Mr. Lenhart just watched it from above. He had given up his day job and had nothing else to do, except to become a grouchy old man. When children squealed in the pool, he screamed at them from his perch. When someone did not park his car properly, he got upset. In the later years, it became difficult not to get into an argument with him.

The strangest thing, however, was that the Lenharts never went down to the beach. Once we forced Mrs. Lenhart to go with us.

"It's too sandy for me," she said and went laughing back home. He had never been to the beach as long as they lived there, never experiencing the different moods of the ocean. For me, the ocean was most exciting when it was rough. The sky dark grey, the water black, the high waves with their bright white crests racing toward the beach, roaring like lions spraying water in the air, an awesome sight. The sea is in a rage. "Don't come near me or I'll swallow you," is the clear message. The next day the sky and water can be blue. The ocean looks like a beautiful large lake. That look can be deceiving. And I have been deceived. We were in Rockaway when my daughter Ellen was two years old. The ocean was very quiet. Everyone went into the water. I carried Ellen on one arm and went in too. Suddenly I saw Ernst running toward us waving his arms wildly. Through the corner of my eye I saw a huge wave coming. I could not get away. I pressed Ellen with both my arms against my body. I was thrown forward. We were both under water. I landed on my knees, holding on to Ellen, keeping her above the ground. Ernst had also been thrown by the wave, as was everyone else. I stood up. He took the crying child from me. My legs were shaking. My knees were bleeding. I stumbled to the beach and fell down. My whole body was shivering. Ellen was very frightened but unhurt. She did not go near the water for a year.

243

I like the ocean best with manageable waves. Waves you can play with, dive into, jump up with, or let them push you towards the beach. That's what we did in school, always under strict supervision. I cannot think about Montauk without comparing it to Juist.

One thing we never did in Montauk was fish. The subject just never came up. But Ernst decided to go deep-sea fishing in Montauk one day. He came home with a catch, a big bluefish. He was very proud. I was very unhappy. We gave it to the Lenharts for their freezer and were promptly invited to a fish dinner.

In Juist we walked the beach a lot in our free time, finding starfish in all sizes and colors from pink to dark red, shells from sea urchins and blue and white jellyfish. The blue ones were harmless, however the sting of the big white ones could really make you sick. When they were lying dead on the beach the boys would throw them at us.

My family and friends learned to love to walk on the beach too. One friend once asked me, "Do you make everybody walk on the beach?" My granddaughter, Daniella, learned to count in German on these walks. Ellen mostly searched for driftwood.

Memorial Day of 1996, Ellen and Daniella went down to the beach even before unpacking their suitcases.

The next morning we went down to the beach together. We always start our walks going against the wind, which mostly comes from the West. On the first day our goal is Gurneys Inn, a forty minute round trip. Our walks get longer day by day until we reach the campsite, which is an hour and a half back and forth. We look for treasures, pretty shells and beach glass. Beach glass comes in different colors: brown, green, aqua and a beautiful blue and purple. The blue and purple is the most precious because they are the rarest. We don't do anything with them, just save them. But I did once see a necklace at an arts and crafts fair with a sign that read "beach glass."

Ten years ago the Lenharts sold their cottages to individual buyers. The new owner of number 4 painted the beautiful wood walls white. The furniture is now modern and so are the pictures on the walls. However, we plan to make reservations for number 4 again next year. It is not the same without the Lenharts — their love for the place and their idiosyncrasies gave it its special flavor — but the beach is the same. To this day when I go down the first day and start walking against the wind with my feet testing the water, I think of Juist.

SIXTY-FIVE PLUS

The day had finally arrived. I had reached the age where I could have all kinds of privileges like paying half fare on buses and subways. I had mixed feelings about that privilege particularly when I used public transportation with someone who did not know my age, which was everyone except my immediate family. Why did I have to advertise how old I was? When I took the bus with someone, I paid the full fare. I gladly paid the extra money to appear young. It took me quite a while to come to my senses. If they knew I was sixty-five would that change the friendship? A woman of sixty-five or any other age smells just as sweet.

At sixty-eight I did not care who was with me, I paid half fare. They might think me sixty-five and I would be three years ahead of the game. Of course, I could have waited until I was seventy then I would have been five years ahead, but the fare went up and the savings were bigger.

There was actually a boon to this tragic new status. Sometimes the bus driver would ask for proof of age, which I took as a big compliment. It made my day! Maybe I could have it both ways, pay half fare and still not look like a bona fide senior citizen. Now there was a consolation. I have to confess, however, that lately I have not been asked for proof of age.

When I was a child I could hardly wait for my birthdays to come around. By the time I was thirteen, I prayed to be sixteen soon. I don't remember what was supposed to happen once I reached this magic age but I do know that nothing changed overnight.

Nothing of course was any different either when my sixty-fifth birthday came around except I had not exactly prayed for it to come.

I suppose now I should count my blessings instead of my birthdays; half fare on public transportation, discounts on air fares, hotels and movies, who could ask for anything more?

At this point I wish birthdays did not exist. I've had enough of them; in fact so many I can hardly count them…and I don't want to either! If nobody remembered my birthday, then nobody would know that I am a year older, except me and the Social Security Agency and maybe the State Department, which mailed me a new passport recently. I mean after all it is a man-made idea to remind people of their age on a yearly basis. And by now I've had it. I can get into any movie without proof of age, I can even buy alcohol and cigarettes, so why do I have to be reminded that I too am mortal? And how about: "Hey, you are catching up with me!" or "How does it feel to reach the big "O"? Whatever "O" that might be every ten years. Sometimes they are even a year ahead of you. "Aren't you lucky you only have to pay half the fare on the bus?" Very lucky indeed!

BACK TO BERLIN AND JUIST 2002

My *Reisefieber* (anxiety before starting a trip) was starting — it was July 22nd, and my daughter Ellen and I were leaving on the 24th for Berlin and Juist. A trip of nostalgia: to Berlin my hometown and to Juist, the island in the North Sea where I went to school. I had been back to Berlin three times, but I wanted to go again after the wall came down and it was once more the capital of Germany. And Juist, which I had not seen for more than 60 years.

I got more excited and tense by the hour. I am always tense before a trip — any trip — but this one was special — more exciting and more emotional.

I did not know what to expect, particularly in Juist where I had spent my entire adolescence seventy years ago.

Ellen was eager to go too. She had heard so much about the school, especially about the beach. Every time we went to Montauk, I would say, "The beach is beautiful here, but the beach in Juist was nicer."

"How do you know? You haven't been there in over sixty years."

"I know, I remember."

We arrived in Berlin on July 25th. Robin, Ellen's friend, picked us up with two beautiful roses. We took a taxi to the Heinrich Heine Hotel on Heinrich Heine Platz. Nothing looked familiar to me on the ride to the hotel. I had never been in this part of the city. I felt like a tourist, a feeling that did not leave me during this entire stay in my hometown.

The taxi driver could not find the hotel on Heinrich Heine Platz, and neither could we. It turned out that you could not drive to the hotel. The street leading to it had cement barriers and was not open for cars. I did not want to think about what they would do in an emergency. So we pulled our heavy suitcases to the hotel on foot and were pleasantly surprised by our accommodations. We had a suite, a big living room, a small bedroom and a little kitchen, which I had no intention of using.

On the corner of Heinrich Heine Platz was a little Italian restaurant where Robin, Ellen and I had dinner. It practically became our hangout; of the five evenings we spent in Berlin, we ate three times in this little place, including our last night when we and the host were sorry to part.

I was in Berlin but it did not feel like it. I could have been in any German town. There was nothing Berlinese about the neighborhood.

Ellen had done some research before we left and knew about places of particular interest to Jews. We decided to go to the Jewish Museum the first morning. Before entering we had a cup of coffee in a "Steh Café" (standing up café) and talked to a German couple. They were in Berlin on their vacation and did not want to miss this museum. They were not Jewish — in fact as much as we could judge most of the people in the museum were Germans and not Jews.

It is a somber place. The walls outside and inside are all gray. The windows are small and narrow and look like slits randomly cut into walls. It is a very sophisticated museum, designed by the Jewish architect Daniel Liebeskind. He lived in Israel and New York and has now made Berlin his home. A U.S. citizen, he is one of six architects selected to study the future of the World Trade Center space, and the one whose design was finally selected.

We started on the first floor, which tells the history of the Jews in Germany. There were pictures of famous people like Einstein and Mendelssohn and short film clips of cities where Jews used to live. We walked through gray corridors and came to a space called "void." Before us was a stream of stylized metal masks. Thousands of them. They represented people of different ages: adults,

smaller ones of children and still smaller ones of infants. All had
their mouths wide open. It looked to me like a stream of screaming people who were slowly squeezed forward while the stream
became narrower and narrower until they disappeared into a black
hole. The masks did not actually move. But as I stood there mesmerized, I saw them being shoved into this black hole screaming.
I stood motionless staring at them. There were a few other people
in this small room —nobody uttered a sound.

The second floor of the museum is dedicated to the recent
history of the Jews in Germany. I did not want to see any pictures
of the Nazi era. I could still see the screaming faces pushed into
the black hole all the way back to the hotel.

We went to an old synagogue (Oranienburgerst) that had been
bombed during the war. The front half of it was rebuilt, and services are held there regularly. Barricades and police guard it
twenty-four hours a day. Next to it is a big kosher restaurant where
we had dinner. I had a plate of Matjes herring and different kinds
of smoked fish. It was delicious, particularly the Matjes herring. It
became my daily lunch. It is not salty and it is as soft as butter.

The other thing I loved was our daily mid-morning coffee
break, which we took wherever we went, and it was always a trip
from our hotel, usually by taxi; in fact, I spent more money on
taxis in Berlin than in the last ten years in New York. We always
sat outside, watching the people go by as well as the many street
artists. It gave me a real feeling of being in Europe but not particularly in Berlin. I had to remind myself that I was actually in
my hometown.

We went to the "Bayrische Viertel." In this beautiful residential area built around a little park, everything was green, the park,
and the many trees along the small quiet streets. Between the trees
and on the sidewalk were posts like lampposts, which had signs on
them. Each one quoted a law that came out during the Nazi era
and the date it was enforced. One said, "Aryan children are not
allowed to play with Jewish children"; this post stood in front of a
playground. Others instructed Jews to hand over their jewelry and
fur coats, or announced that Jewish people or persons married to
Jews cannot work for the post office anymore, or that Aryans are
not allowed to go to Jewish doctors…and many, many more. There

were supposed to be eighty of these signs but we did not find them all. Who reads them, I don't know. I also don't know by whom they were put up.

On a wall of a newly renovated building we found the names of the Jewish families who used to live there. It was across the street from an old Jewish cemetery that had been, except for two graves, completely destroyed. We quietly put a small rock on each gravestone.

But I also wanted to go to the Kadewe, the department store in Berlin. I remembered it from before I left Germany and from my last visit to this city when I bought two beautiful sweaters for my granddaughter Daniella there. This time it was swarming with people, like Macy's on Christmas Eve. We didn't buy anything and got out fast. The Kadewe is opposite Wittenberg Platz, a small square in this very busy shopping area with a busy subway station. In front of the subway entrance stood a post that was hard to overlook.

On top it said, "*Orte des Schreckens die wir niemals vergessen duerfen*" (Places of terror which we should never forget), underneath on individual signs were the names of concentration camps, twelve of them. I read them all. Not all the names were familiar to me. But Auschwitz certainly was; it was from there that I received the last letter from my parents via the Red Cross. I was upset reading all those names but I was also pleased that the post was there, visible to everyone. Ellen took a picture of the sign and then we hailed a taxi.

To my pleasant surprise, Ellen spoke German very well. She asked the taxi driver what he thought of the sign.

"It's enough already," he said. "Now they want to build a Holocaust Memorial Unter den Linden. It will cost twenty-five million Euros, it is ridiculous. I read a book written by a Jewish doctor, he says that two million Jews survived. Where did they come from if six million were killed? And the Jewish mafia got all the reparation money!"

"Not true," said Ellen.

"I got my money," I said.

"How much did you get?"

"None of your business!" What was this? An interrogation? I was trembling and wanted to get out of the car but I didn't. Instead I said, "My entire family was killed in Auschwitz, stop already!"

But he did not seem to hear me and kept on raving about the money that was wasted and the Jewish mafia. I was shaking now and screamed, "*Schluss*!" (stop). That shut him up. He drove us silently to Heinrich Heine Platz. When we got out of the car Ellen said to him, "Maybe you should read another book; one isn't enough."

We walked slowly to the hotel. I was still shaking and thought: this was a young man born long after the war, where does his hate come from? It was my first personal encounter with a Nazi. I shook my head and thought of course there are Nazis in Germany and not only in Germany but they are in every country. But I had never run into one before — never.

The next morning we went to the Postdamer Platz, the Times Square of Berlin before the war. Its pride then was a tower in the middle of the square from which a policeman regulated the traffic. The famous square became no-man's land after Germany was divided among the victorious powers.

Huge new buildings, American style, surround the busy square today. They all have glass fronts and look majestic. In the middle of the square the little traffic tower still stands, unused, as a memento. It was the only thing that looked familiar to me. The Postdamer Platz is again the center of the city with heavy traffic and hundreds of people milling around. On this particular day most of them were admiring a big photo exhibit. We admired it too. The pictures were landscapes from all over the world taken by photographers from all over the world. They were very large and in beautiful colors. Fields of corn, forests, deserts, towns and more.

After our usual coffee break we hopped into a taxi and drove to Unter den Linden, a very wide boulevard, which starts at the Brandenburger Tor and ends at the Statsoper, the biggest opera house in Berlin. We walked from end to end. I was looking for a café on this famous street where Ernst, some helpful friends and I met the day before he left Germany in 1938. The next morning, he and his mother and brother departed for Holland. I couldn't find the cafe.

Our stay in Berlin was too short. With the exception of a small Kaethe Kollwitz exhibit we did not get into any of the interesting museums in Berlin. I would like to come back, stay longer, walk through it at leisure and find some familiar places to get nostalgic about. I did not enjoy feeling like a tourist in Berlin. I wanted to believe it was my hometown, but it did not feel like it. Nothing felt like home — everything was new or strange.

July 30th was our departure date for Juist. I ordered a taxi to get us to the station the night before. The driver came to the hotel to help us with the luggage. Going up to the platform at the station with my heavy suitcase I fell on the escalator. I could not get up. Ellen screamed, *"Hilfe!"* (Help). A young woman helped me up and a man took hold of my suitcases. I was okay but we were both in shock. What next, I thought?

We had to change trains in Hanover. Our car to that city was air-conditioned, a very pleasant surprise because despite the heat in Berlin nothing was air-conditioned, neither the hotel nor any restaurants. In Hanover, my German friends, Friederike and her mother Marianne joined us. We all boarded the train to Nordeik where we had to catch the boat to Juist. This train was not air-conditioned, and a local to boot. The heat was unbearable and the open windows did not help. After a torturous three-hour ride we arrived in Nordeik where the sea breeze revived us.

The boat to Juist was waiting and we boarded to begin our two-hour trip to the island. It was crowded. The last time I had made the trip was in January 1933. The sea was rough then, the boat much smaller, and the passengers were mostly students from the Schule am Meer. We always became excited as we got closer to Juist and could see the school buildings in the distance. But this time I was unable to recognize the school. There were buildings all over, houses that had not existed in 1933. For a moment I thought we were on the wrong boat. Then it hit me that 1933 was a long time ago — everything will be different. I might as well get used to it.

We docked right at the island. The little train that used to connect the boat to Juist did not exist anymore. We always had so much fun on that slow little train, particularly when we jumped off and on while it was moving.

There are still no cars on Juist, only bicycles and horse drawn carriages. We walked to the hotel. The next morning we hired a carriage to get us to the area where the school used to be. The dirt road through the dunes was now a brick road lined with clean brick houses of all sizes. Private homes and guesthouses. Colorful flowers decorated the balconies and the little lawns. There was no dune in sight and nothing looked familiar to me. The carriage ride seemed to take a long time. We used to walk the dirt road faster, I thought.

When we finally arrived at the designated area we were surrounded by brick buildings old and new. I looked around and recognized three school buildings: the music hall and then the Ark where I had lived in my last three years, and the Diesseits, where the dining room and the kitchen used to be. We went into the music hall. Little children were running around making a lot of noise. The big hall was divided by a partition and was unrecognizable. It turned out to be a children's camp. The school was gone! I was in a strange place. I tried to reconstruct it with the help of the remaining buildings and described it to Ellen and my friends but I did not succeed. Now I was eager to get to the little museum Marianne had told me about. She had been there on her last visit to the island and had seen pictures of the school exhibited. But there were no pictures of the Schule am Meer now. We asked the woman in charge. She had never heard of it.

"You have never heard about the Schule am Meer?"

"No, I am only here three months."

"They had pictures of the school here," Marianne said.

"I really don't know about that." And then she picked up the phone, called a Mr. Kolde, and handed the phone to me. He knew about the school and we met that afternoon in my hotel. Mr. Kolde was trying to get money to add a room about the school to the museum. He had papers and photo albums with familiar pictures and the original registration forms of every student, including mine with a picture that I would never have recognized. He told me that in the village the school was called "die Judenschule." I was shocked - I had never heard that before. In fact there were only two Jewish teachers and very few Jewish students in the school. We had no contact with people in the village except on very rare occasions with the physician. I will never find out why they called it the Judenschule, but it does not make me feel good.

The Schule am Meer was only in existence for nine years. It was closed in 1934, one year after I left, not only because of the Nazis, Mr. Kolde said, but also because it ran out of money. Financially it had been totally mismanaged, which I had not known either.

In sum, my meeting with Mr. Kolde was interesting but also upsetting. The fact is that nothing remains of my school where I had spent so many happy years.

The buildings that did remain could have been anywhere, there was no aura around them. However, I can remember the joy and spirit that was in those buildings. I don't have to go back to Juist for it.

The island has become a beautiful resort, with fancy hotels, fancy stores, little restaurants and cafes, no cars and very clean streets. The only thing unchanged is the beach. It is just as wide and white and clean as I remembered it. Walking on it again was a thrill. Even Ellen had to concede that it is more beautiful than Montauk's. I had walked on that beach hundreds of times during the day and at night when the moon eerily gave the sand a grayish blue color. Now it was covered with vacationers, beach chairs and little children building sandcastles. You could see the yellow umbrellas of a restaurant on the boardwalk — a boardwalk that nobody even dreamed of in my time. Ellen and I and our friends had our lunches under the yellow umbrellas too and I ordered my delicious Matjes herring every time.

August 3rd was our departure day. Marianne and Friederike were off to Hanover, Ellen to Duesseldorf to visit a friend, and I was going to Bad Reichenhall.

We had decided to fly back to the mainland. It was the only way to catch our train, which left early in the morning from

Nordeik. The evening before it was foggy and Marianne, speaking from experience, said, "if it is foggy they won't fly."

"What, they won't fly? We planned this trip for nearly a year and they won't fly?" I was hysterical with laughter. "How will we make our connections? The boat only leaves in the afternoon, we can't swim to Nordeik!"

Frederike chimed in, "I've got to get home, we are leaving for Iceland in two days!"

Now we were all laughing hysterically and finally decided that there simply would not be any fog on an August morning.

At 7 a.m. sharp, a covered wagon pulled by two big horses stood in front of our hotel to get us to the plane. Another couple joined us. For half an hour the horses pulled us slowly on a brick covered road through the dunes. The ride seemed endless. It was a unique way to get to an airport. The little plane was standing in the middle of nowhere, waiting for us. Before we could board, we had to pay our fare, 33 Euros per person, to a woman in a wooden hut. That little hut was the extent of the airport in Juist.

The little flying machine was filled to capacity by the six of us. It took exactly ten minutes to get to Nordeik and that includes going up and landing.

We made our train. Ellen and I had to change in Bremen. She was off to Dusseldorf, and I had to get a plane to Frankfurt in order to catch yet another plane for Salzburg. There a car from my hotel met me and took me to my destination, Bad Reichenhall. A long and tiring day! I was looking forward to my two weeks rest in this lovely little town.

But after two weeks I had rested enough and was eager to get home. As usual, I was tense the day I left but relaxed the minute I got on the plane to New York. Driving home in the taxi from Kennedy airport, I saw the familiar skyline of New York. It looked particularly beautiful in the setting sun. Every time I see it I marvel at the beauty of it and remember how Ernst and I felt when we saw it for the first time, coming into New York Harbor in 1939. Happy to have reached our destination, sad thinking about the people we left behind, and uneasy about what to expect. This time I felt happy to be welcomed home by it.

While I felt for a long time that Berlin was my hometown, I never thought about moving back to that city. In my nostalgia I felt the way it was before Hitler came to power. I wanted to turn the clock back. That, of course, was a fantasy, too. Going back to it, I realized not only that I didn't belong there anymore, but also that I was glad I could go home, home to New York.

No, I am not a Berliner anymore. But I had to go back to realize the truth: I am a New Yorker now. I had actually been a New Yorker for some time; I just had to get the nostalgia fantasy out of my system. And I did.